101 828 838 4

KT-417-118

COMMUNITY

ONE WEEK LOAN

KEY IDEAS

Series Editor: PETER HAMILTON, The Open University, Milton Keynes

Designed to complement the successful *Key Sociologists*, this series covers the main concepts, issues, debates, and controversies in sociology and the social sciences. The series aims to provide authoritative essays on central topics of social science, such as community, power, work, sexuality, inequality, benefits and ideology, class, family, etc. Books adopt a strong individual 'line' constituting original essays rather than literary surveys, and lively and original treatments of their subject matter. The books will be useful to students and teachers of sociology, political science, economics, psychology, philosophy, and geography.

COMMUNITY

Gerard Delanty

Routledge
Taylor & Francis Group

LONDON AND NEW YORK

First published 2003
by Routledge
2 Park Square, Milton Park, Abingdon Oxon OX14 4RN

Simultaneously published in the USA and Canada
by Routledge
270 Madison Ave, New York, NY 10016

Reprinted 2003, 2004, 2005, 2006

Routledge is an imprint of the Taylor & Francis Group, an informa business

© 2003 Gerard Delanty

Typeset in Garamond by
Keystroke, Jacaranda Lodge, Wolverhampton
Printed and bound in Great Britain by
TJ International Ltd, Padstow, Cornwall

British Library Cataloguing in Publication Data
A catalogue record for this book is available from the British Library

Library of Congress Cataloging in Publication Data
A catalog record for this book has been requested

ISBN10: 0–415–23685–1 (hbk)
ISBN10: 0–415–23686–X (pbk)

ISBN13: 978–0–415–23685–0 (hbk)
ISBN13: 978–0–415–23686–7 (pbk)

'Never was the word "community" used more indiscriminately and emptily than in the decades when communities in the sociological sense became hard to find in real life.'
Eric Hobsbawm *The Age of Extremes* (1994, p. 428)

'On each side of the political spectrum today we see a fear of social disintegration and a call for a revival of community.'
Anthony Giddens *Beyond Left and Right* (1994, p. 124)

'We miss community because we miss security, a quality crucial to a happy life, but one which the world we inhabit is ever less able to offer and ever more reluctant to promise.'
Zygmunt Bauman *Community* (2001, p. 144)

'A communitarian society is suffocating and can be transformed into a theocratic or nationalist despotism.'
Alain Touraine *Critique of Modernity* (1995, p. 304).

'Community life can be understood as the life people live in dense, multiplex, relatively autonomous networks of social relationships. Community, thus, is not a place or simply a small-scale population aggregate, but a mode of relating, variable in extent.'
Craig Calhoun *Sociological Inquiry* (1998, vol. 68, no 3, p. 381)

'Perhaps the necessary analytical step to understanding the new forms of social interaction in the age of the Internet is to build on a definition of community, de-emphasizing its cultural component, emphasizing its supportive role to individuals and families, and de-linking its social existence.'
Manuel Castells *The Internet Galaxy* (2001, p. 127)

'The morality of a community not only lays down how its members should act: it also provides grounds for the consensual resolution of relevant conflicts.'
Jürgen Habermas *The Inclusion of the Other* (1998, p. 4)

Contents

INTRODUCTION

This book aims to give a contemporary interpretation of the idea of community. The point of departure for this assessment of what has been one of the traditional concepts in sociology is the recognition that community is currently in transition as a result of important social, cultural and political developments. Some of the major transformations in the world today are having a huge impact on the idea of community, which has become a highly topical issue in recent social and political thought. The concept of community in classical sociology and community studies has been challenged by developments relating to postmodernism, globalization, the Internet and 'third-way'-style politics. Far from disappearing, as the classical sociologists believed, community has a contemporary resonance in the current social and political situation, which appears to have produced a worldwide search for roots, identity and aspirations for belonging.

The idea of community, which perhaps explains its enduring appeal, is related to the search for belonging in the insecure conditions of modernity. The popularity of community today can be seen as a response to the crisis in solidarity and belonging that has been exacerbated and at the same time induced by globalization. Modernity produced three major upheavals, which gave rise to the main discourses of community: the American and French revolutions, industrialization from the end of the nineteenth century, and the present age of globalization. The many expressions of community that have derived from these and other developments have varied from alternative and utopian communities to traditional villages and urban localities in industrial cities to transnational diasporas and virtual communities. Communities have been based on ethnicity, religion, class or politics; they may be large or small; 'thin' or 'thick' attachments may underlie them; they may be locally based and globally organized; affirmative or subversive in their relation to the established order; they may be traditional, modern and even postmodern; reactionary and progressive.

Social and political scientists, historians and philosophers have been divided on their use of the term *community*, leading many to question its usefulness. But virtually every term in social science is contested, and if we reject the word *community* we will have to replace it with another term. In general, for sociologists community has traditionally designated a particular form of social organization based on small groups, such as neighbourhoods, the small town, or a spatially bounded locality. Anthropologists have applied it to culturally defined groups. In other usages, community refers to political community, where the emphasis is on citizenship, self-government, civil society and collective identity. Philosophical and historical studies have focused more on the idea of community as an ideology or utopia.

Anthony Cohen argued in his well known book *The Symbolic Structure of Community* that community is to be understood as less a social practice than a symbolic structure (Cohen, 1985). Cohen's argument has been very influential in debates on community in the last two decades and tended to shift the focus away from the older emphasis on community as form of social interaction based on locality to a concern with meaning and identity. This generally cultural approach was also reflected in the very influential book by Benedict Anderson, *Imaginary Communities* (Anderson, 1983). Although Anderson's book was primarily concerned with national identity, his approach tended to have a broader influence on community as 'imagined' rather than as a specific form of social interaction. Indeed, the whole point of Anderson's study was to show that community is shaped by cognitive and symbolic structures that are not underpinned by 'lived' spaces and immediate forms of social intimacy. In the view of many critics this led to a loss of the social dimension of community and an excessive concern with the cultural dimension (Amit, 2002). This inevitably led to a view of community as shaped by what separates people rather than by what they have in common. It is this view of community that has been questioned today by critics who want to reinsert the social into community and recover the sense of place that was displaced by the cultural turn in the theory of community.

These different uses of the term are unavoidable. However, a closer look reveals that the term *community* does in fact designate both an idea about belonging and a particular social phenomenon, such as expressions of longing for community, the search for meaning and solidarity, and collective identities. In other words, community has a variable nature and cannot simply be equated with particular groups or a place. Nor can it be reduced to an idea, for ideas do not simply exist outside social relations, socially structured discourses and a historical milieu.

Looking at these debates we find four broad positions that are not easily reconcilable given their respective concerns with social, cultural, political and technological issues. First, there is an approach typical of community studies but also reflected in communitarian philosophy which associates community with disadvantaged urban localities and requiring government-supported responses and civic voluntarism such as community regeneration, community health projects, etc. Here, 'community' is highly spatialized and has to be helped by the mainstream 'society'. A second approach is characteristic of cultural sociology and anthropology where community is seen as the search for belonging and where the emphasis is on cultural issues of identity. In this approach, the emphasis is on community as Self versus Other. The third position on community is inspired by post-modern politics and radical democracy and looks at community in terms of political consciousness and collective action. In this approach, the emphasis is on the collective We opposing injustice. A fourth but less clear-cut position has more recently emerged around global communications, transnational movements and the Internet whereby community becomes cosmopolitanized and constituted in new relations of proximity and distance. In this development, technology plays a key role in reshaping social relations beyond the traditional categories of place. If anything unites these very diverse conceptions of community it is the idea that community concerns belonging.

The approach adopted in this book will be to interpret community in the way it has been used by the various schools of thought. It is only by taking a broad and interdisciplinary look at the idea of community in modern social and political thought that we can have a fuller understanding of the significance of current developments. The structure of the book reflects this view which points to an interdisciplinary approach entailing perspectives in political philosophy, sociology, anthropology and history. The chapters trace the shift from classical conceptions of community in philosophy and social science towards the contemporary situation. This is the story of the rise, decline and rebirth of community. The nineteenth century – but going back to the Christian tradition – was the century of community, while the discourses of the twentieth century have on the whole been ones of the crisis of community. From the final decades of the twentieth century and the beginning of this century community has been revived, as is reflected in communitarianism, recent postmodern thought, theories of cosmopolitanism and transnationalism.

In Chapter 1 some of the historical expressions of community in western thought and politics are discussed. Our concern here is largely with the utopian vision of community as a radical alternative to the prevailing order. It will be shown that in history the idea of community has taken a variety of forms, ranging from subversive aspirations to conservative affirmations of the status quo.

Chapter 2 looks at the idea of community in classical sociology and anthropology, especially around debates on the decline of community with the coming of modernity. Consideration is given to Tönnies' famous work on community and society, Durkheim's sociology of civic community and Victor Turner's symbolic community.

Chapter 3 shifts the emphasis from cultural and political conceptions of community to community in urban sociology and community studies. The chapter deals with the theme of local community in the Chicago School approaches and in more recent urban social theory. This, too, is largely a story of the decline of community under the conditions of modernization and, more lately, globalization.

Chapter 4 deals with the resurgence of community in communitarian thought. In this context the idea of political community is returned to, but this time with the emphasis on the question of belonging as an expression of citizenship.

Chapter 5 turns to the specific question of multiculturalism and the conflict of different conceptions of cultural community. Ten models of multiculturalism are looked at under the headings of traditional multiculturalism, modern multiculturalism and post-multiculturalism.

Chapter 6 moves on to discuss the emergence of radical kinds of community as associated with social movements. In this context the idea of communication communities is introduced. The chapter explores the relation between community and individualism in the light of new conceptions of individualism.

Chapter 7 presents a critical discussion of the main postmodern theories of community and explores the idea of community beyond unity. Examples of this are taken from everyday life, New Age travellers and communities of taste.

Chapter 8 introduces the question of cosmopolitan community in the sense of community beyond the nation-state, in particular in the context of globalization. It looks at different expressions of this around debates on world community and transnational communities.

Chapter 9 looks at one of the most important conceptions of community today, namely virtual community. The main theories are critically assessed with a view to making sense of how technologically mediated forms of interaction constitute a form of community.

I am grateful to three readers who wrote reports on the outline for the book. I am especially grateful to two readers who read the draft of the manuscript and made very useful recommendations for the completion of the final version. Thanks are also due to Mari Shullaw at Routledge for her helpful advice.

1

COMMUNITY AS AN IDEA
Loss and recovery

To understand the appeal of the idea of community we need to go back far into the early origins of modern thought. According to Robert Nisbet in *The Sociological Tradition*, 'Much of the reorientation of moral and social philosophy is the consequence of the impact of the rediscovery of community in historical and sociological thought' (Nisbet, 1967, p. 53).

While today community is often and, as I shall argue, incorrectly seen in opposition to society and based on non-contractual ties, in earlier times this was not the case. Indeed, community was often highly political and even contractual. For Aristotle there was no essential difference between the social and the communal, since the idea of society was associated with friendship. The polis of classical Greece contained within it political, social and economic relations. Aristotle in fact saw the city – the polis – as a community (*koinonia*) which for him had a very urban character, a contrast to the tribal and rural social relations of arcadia. The communal forms of the Greek city produce contractual ties in which the social character of people reaches its highest level. For this reason the romantic and nostalgic distinction made in the nineteenth century of a golden age of community preceding the advent of society is highly questionable as a description of community before modernity.[1]

From the ancient Greeks to the Enlightenment community expressed the essence of society, not its antithesis. For Rousseau in the eighteenth century modern civil society was based on the Greek polis as an association of citizens. In the Enlightenment the idea of community encapsulated the emerging world of society. Reducible to neither the state nor to the private world of the household, community expressed bonds of commonality and sociality. Insofar as community expressed a domain of specifically social relations, it indicated a tension with the autocratic state. In contrast to the state, community referred to the more immediate world of meaning, belonging and everyday life. While the state was an objective and distant entity far removed from people's lives, community was something directly experienced. In early modern thought community and society were virtually interchangeable: community designated the social domain of the 'life-world', the lived world of everyday life. Although these spheres were to become more and more bifurcated, in the seventeenth and eighteenth centuries both could express much the same concern. This interchangeability of community and society may be seen in the idea of civil society. Until the late nineteenth century there was no clear definition of the social as a reality *sui generis*, as Durkheim was to claim. Instead society was seen as the civic bond, which could refer also to economic relations as opposed to political relations. Civil society could also be expressed in terms of the common bond, or community. Community thus did not mean merely tradition but simply social relations, such as those that were in fact emerging around a market-based society and bourgeois culture.

Raymond Williams has outlined how the earlier idea of society was felt to be more immediate than it later became, and to this extent it meant much the same as the idea of community (Williams, 1976, p. 75). His suggestion is that the idea of community inherited from the early idea of society the body of direct relationships as opposed to the organized realm of the state. While the idea of society progressively lost this sense of the immediacy of direct relationships, the notion of community retained it and continued to be the word used to designate such experiments in alternatives to the status quo. Robert Nisbet reflected this kind of thinking when he claimed that sociology has always conceived the social as the communal:

> Sociology, above any other discipline in the [twentieth] century, gave primacy to the concept of the social. The point to be emphasized here, however, is that the referent of the 'social' was almost invariably the communal. *Communitas*, not *societas* with its more impersonal connotations, is the real etymological source of the sociologist's use of the word 'social' in his studies of personality, kinship, economy, and polity.
>
> (Nisbet, 1967, p. 56)

We can make a more general observation on the basis of this interchangeability of the terms *society* and *community* in an earlier period in the formation of modernity. The defining element in the discourse of community from the seventeenth century onwards was a critique of the state, which in the age of the Enlightenment was absolutist. In this respect community expressed a dream impossible to realize: a vision of a pure or pristine social bond that did not need a state. It was in a sense a purely utopian concept of community. The ideal of community in western thought has been much animated by the vision of a society without a state, or rather without the need for a state. Much of modern thought has seen the state either as the enemy of the social, a kind of necessary evil as in liberalism, or as something to be abolished. Anarchism, Freemasonry, liberalism and civic republicanism have all been defined in opposition to the state. Socialism has regarded the state as a stepping stone to communism, for which the state is the expression of human alienation. Exceptions to this are modern conservatism, Zionism and nationalism which have looked to the state as a model for defining the social. In these ideologies the state has generally been seen as an organic entity expressing the totality of political community. We return to the question of political ideology and community below, but for now the point that needs to be established is that by the nineteenth century community came to embody the quest for a perfect society. For the early moderns – as in the political theory of Thomas Hobbes – the state was a Leviathan, a monstrous creature necessary for the survival of society but which had to be subdued and, in many of the discourses of modernity, abolished. Community thus points to an organic conception of the social as encompassing political, civic and social relations. What is important here is the immediate and experiential aspect of community as embodying direct relationships in contrast to the alien world of the state. The tendency always existed for community to be a challenge to the state, and in many cases even an alternative. Today in the global age, with international terror on the rise, religious militancy and new nationalisms, community as a total critique of the state has been revitalized.

But of course no society can exist without a state. The quest for community must be seen as a perpetual critique of the state that is utopian in its inspiration. There are two aspects to this. Community is seen as something that has been lost with modernity and as something that must be recovered. As a process dominated by state formation, modernity has allegedly destroyed community. Modernity has taken politics out of the social and confined the political to the state. It is in opposition to this that community as a vision of society purified of the state has received its animus. As a discourse of loss and recovery, community can be utopian and at the same time nostalgic. The modernist assumption has been that community once existed and has been destroyed by the modern world which has been erected on different foundations. In Chapter 2, the nostalgic dimension is discussed in more detail. In this chapter, we concentrate on the utopian aspect of community as a discourse of both loss and recovery. It will suffice for present purposes to point out that the nostalgic narrative of loss has given the utopian dream its basic direction. It has also been the source of some of the greatest political dangers, giving rise to the myth of the total community that has fuelled fundamentalist, nationalist and fascist ideologies in the twentieth century. With is promise of a better future, community has been subversive of modernity, seeking a recovery of the social and politics.

In this chapter we look at some of the major historical discourses of community in western thought and political practice. We begin with the rise of the ideal of community in the encounter of Greek and Christian thought. Second, from ancient thought we move on to the discourse of loss that began with the decline of the institutions of the Middle Ages. Third, modernity and utopian political ideology is discussed as a foundation of community, which is not only a discourse of loss but also one of recovery and realization. Fourth, the idea of total community is discussed as embodied in fascist political ideology on the one side and on the other in radical communal movements. If these very different conceptions of community have anything in common, it is a view of community as *communitas*, to use the Latin term, as an expression of belonging that is irreducible to any social or political arrangement. Community exerts itself as a powerful idea of belonging in every age, and as such its reality consists of its persuasive power as the most 'social' aspect of society.

COMMUNITY BETWEEN POLIS AND COSMOS

Lying at the heart of the idea of community is an ambivalence. On the one side, it expresses locality and particularness – the domain of immediate social relations, the familiar, proximity – and, on the other, it refers to the universal community in which all human beings participate. This double sense of community, all the more acute today with cosmopolitanism at the forefront of political debate, has always been central to the idea of community. Community can be exclusive or inclusive. For Parsons the highest expression of social integration was the 'societal community' (Parsons, 1961, p. 10). In other and more post-traditional forms, for instance, the European Community (the earlier name of the European Union) or virtual communities (to be discussed in Chapter 9), community is an expression of global humanity. In contrast, for Ferdinand Tönnies community was the basis of social integration and expressed traditional face-to-face relations of a non-contractual nature. Rather than see these conceptions of community as exclusive, it is more fruitful to see them as complementary and with a long history in western political traditions.

It is not an exaggeration to say that the modern idea of community has been deeply influenced by classical thought which bequeathed two conflicting conceptions of community: the human order of the polis and the universal order of the cosmos. These traditions correspond approximately to the Greek and Christian traditions. There can be no doubt that the modern idea of community has its origins in the Greek political community, the polis. The kind of community that was exemplified in the polis provided the basic ideal for all subsequent conceptions of community. It was first of all local, embodying the human dimension of the city as opposed to a larger entity. As such the communitarian order of the polis was one of immediacy. Politics was based on the voice; in its pure form it was indistinguishable from friendship and from participation in public life, which was both an ideal and a practice for the Greeks, who did not know the separation of the social from the political.

According to Hannah Arendt, one of the major interpreters of Greek political thought, the polis ideal asserted the primacy of politics over the social (Arendt, 1958). But this is to be understood as the absence of any distinction between the social and the political. Politics was not confined to the state but was conducted in everyday life in self-government by citizens. The Greeks did not experience the alienation of politics in the state, which Marx claimed was the achievement of capitalism. For this reason, many thinkers – Rousseau, Hegel, Marx, Arendt – admired the Greek polis, which served as a kind of normative critique of modernity. In these critiques, as will be commented on below, we also find the beginnings of the idea of community as a discourse of loss.

It also needs to be pointed out that while the Greek polis may have made politics more immediate, the price that had to be paid was a high degree of exclusion. It appears that the price for the inclusion of some is the exclusion of others. Thus the Greek communitarian ideal of the polis may be seen in a negative light as constructed around strong codes of us/them. However, the main point is that for the Greeks community was to be found in the immediacy of public life. The polis was a contrast to the cosmic order of the gods. Although the Greeks tried to construct the polis to reflect the cosmos, the polis ideal was always in tension with the divine order, the universal order of the cosmopolis. To an extent this divide was overcome by the Romans, who linked *societas* with *universalis*. The Roman Empire itself was to be a universal human community based on citizenship. However, the idea of a universal community that would transcend the territory of the political order did not develop fully until the arrival of Christian thought, especially with Augustine. Where the Greeks gave priority to the polis as the domain of community,

Christian thought stressed the universal community as a communion with the sacred. Augustine, in his *City of God* (413–25), which established the foundations of medieval political theory, outlined how the 'city of man' was incomplete and thus a contrast to the universal community of the 'celestial city' of God which was conceived as a perfect human community but one that could never be realized in human history. The idea of the ecumenicity of the universal Church suggests this wider concept of community as an order that transcends the social and the political. A definition of community in a French dictionary in 1538 stated that the word *community* indicates 'a totality of persons, and abstractly, the condition of what is common to several persons. Applied to persons, it indicates a religious collectivity.'[2]

What emerges from this is a notion of community as participation in a universal order. This concept of community has been very influential in modern times in that it has postulated a far-reaching critique of the human order of society. Community thus enters into tension with society, which it rejects in the name of a higher order. This kind of universal community has been reflected in many of the world religions, not just in Christianity. In Islam there is also to be found such an emphasis on community – the *umma* – as extending beyond the immediate context and embodying a principle of unity.[3] In the Confucian tradition of China community also extends to encompass the cosmic order (Schwartz, 1991). Community is also a powerful discourse in Indian society and its principal religions (Jodhka, 2002).

Thus far we have established that in the critical juncture of Greek and Christian thought two senses of community emerge which are fundamentally contradictory: community as local and therefore particular and, on the other side, community as ultimately universal. This conflict has never been resolved and has endured to the present day when we find two kinds of community in conflict: the cosmopolitan quest for belonging on a global level and the indigenous search for roots.

MODERNITY AND THE LOSS OF COMMUNITY

It has already been noted that the modern discourse of community has been dominated by a theme of loss. As is suggested in the work of many sociologists, such as Ferdinand Tönnies, Max Weber and Robert Nisbet, it was the decline of the institutions of the Middle Ages that led to the sense of the loss of community. The breakup of the medieval guilds and corporations, the commercialization of agriculture that came with the emergence of capitalism and the decline in the autonomy of the cities following the rise of the modern centralized state led to a disenchantment with community. While it was not until the emergence of modern sociology that the theme of the loss of community became fully theorized, modern thought from the Enlightenment onwards was preoccupied with a sense of the passing of an allegedly organic world. Unlike the classicism of the Renaissance, the Enlightenment certainly looked to the positive aspects of modernity on the whole, but even that movement's most characteristic figures tended to see in the present the ruins of the past.

Rousseau, for instance, saw modernity as the alienation of the individual and the loss in political autonomy. An admirer of the classical republican city state, Rousseau was deeply sceptical of the ability of the institutions of modernity to realize community. In particular, he saw the state as destructive of human freedom and political possibilities. In a sense, his notion of the 'general will' suggests the ideal of community. According to Rousseau, who has been widely regarded as one of the founders of modern civic republicanism, the general will is the only genuine form of political organization. In his political philosophy, the human desire for freedom could express itself only in community. The sense of loss is very apparent in this tradition in political philosophy. Community lies at the foundation of politics but it was eroded by modernity which can never recover fully a pure kind of politics uncontaminated by social institutions. Rousseau's conception of community was based on his view of human nature as fundamentally good and in tension with social institutions and structures, such as the state. It was an organic vision of community that was also a critique of modernity. There is not much in Rousseau's thought to suggest that he believed modernity could re-create community based on the general will. In this respect Hegel was different.

Hegel's whole social theory of modernity was conceived in terms of the overcoming of earlier forms of consciousness, beginning with the Greek polis. The Hegelian conception of modernity was one of the failure of modern society to embody in its institutions 'ethical life' (*Sittlichkeit*), a term that approximately – and with some liberty of interpretation – corresponds to the meaning of community as a civic and symbolic entity but which also has a transcendental, normative component.[4] For Hegel, 'ethical life' is perpetually destroyed by modernity and must be rescued on ever higher levels. Thus, the state becomes the highest embodiment of 'ethical life', since society alone, due to its conflicts, cannot sustain itself. This view of the state has led to accusations of totalitarianism, as in Karl Popper's famous attack on Hegel, or the claim that he was a political legitimist of the Prussian state. While there is some justification for these claims in Hegel's often obscure and politically ambivalent writings, a more plausible interpretation is that Hegel was advocating a theory of the state as one of civic community. In this view, community is realizable only in a political form and that, ultimately, there is no essential difference between the level of the political and the social. There is some basis in Hegel's work for the view that he saw the problem of modernity as the problem of community. 'The true state, for Hegel, is a *communitas communitatum* rather than the aggregate of individuals that the Enlightenment had held it to be', wrote Robert Nisbet (1967, p. 55). In Hegelian political philosophy, the political task is to ground the state in the social, but since the social is itself incomplete, only a deeper level of community can guarantee the survival of the political. Thus in contrast to the romantic and radical Rousseau, Hegel did not see community entirely in terms of loss. Yet there is no denying the theme of loss in his thought, which saw history as a struggle to realize what was always contained in older forms of thought. Modernity itself could never escape from this condition, which Hegel described as an 'unhappy consciousness', never fully able to realize itself.

This theme of the loss of the normative ideal of community in modernity has undoubtedly Christian connotations, and, even more deeply, Hebraic roots. John Milton's epic poem of the failure of the English Revolution to realize the Puritan cause is the most famous example of this view of modernity as a narrative of human failure. Cast in the metaphors of the Christian myth, *Paradise Lost* [1667] tells the story of how England's entry to modernity failed to achieve the revolutionary goal of recovering a pristine community. While such an explicitly Christian reading of the failure of modern revolutions is not to be found in the works of the Enlightenment thinkers of the following century, some of the central themes remained. Even in Hegel, for example, the French Revolution is interpreted as a failure because the human actor does not have insight into the deeper historical process by which Reason becomes conscious of itself. So, ulti-mately, in Hegel, community is impossible since it is necessarily incomplete, for only the philosopher has access to true knowledge in the sense of possessing a complete understanding of the historical meaning of an epoch.[5]

COMMUNITY REGAINED: MODERNITY AND ITS UTOPIAS

The theme of loss is only one side to the modern discourse of community. The other side is the theme of the realization of community. Many of the great conceptions of community in western thought were of the recovery of what has been lost. The idea of the loss and recovery of community may be seen as together constituting the millennial tradition in western thought. According to Norman Cohen in *The Pursuit of the Millennium* this tradition has been at the root of much western thought (Cohen, 1970). With its origins in the Hebraic millenarian traditions and Christianity, modernity inherited the aspiration of salvation as a recovery of something lost and which often formed the basis of radical communitarian movements (Kamenka, 1982a). The vision of community was often connected with visions of world catastrophe, but as Victor Turner has argued this was not confined to modernity. 'Apocalyptic *communitas*', he argued, has been part of many primitive cultures and also of medieval Christianity (Turner, 1969, pp. 153–4).

The realization of community has been a theme in some of the most influential universalistic political ideologies of modernity, in particular those that characterized the period from about 1830 to 1989; that is, the era that began following the waning of the Enlightenment to the collapse of communism. In this period, which we will call the Age of Ideology, the doctrines of liberalism, republicanism, conservatism, communism and its variants, socialism and anarchism, Zionism, fascism, and nationalism competed with each other, defining different political and moral visions of society. Lying at the source of all of these programmatic designs were particular conceptions of community as a largely normative ideal. What is peculiar to all this is the utopian imagination. As previously remarked, community is an utopian idea, for it is as much an ideal to be achieved as a reality that concretely exists. It expresses the utopian desire for an alternative to the status quo. The nineteenth century was the age of the proliferation of new communities, especially in America. Communistic communities were very common in nineteenth-century America where the utopian imagination was very strong and frequently took the form of experiments in communism and in alternative conceptions of progress. According to Krishan Kumar, they were the product of a wider movement of reform that embraced socialism (Kumar, 1987, pp. 82–3). The communal movement varied from the sectarian religious movements of the seventeenth century to the communal movements inspired by communism in the nineteenth century to anarchist ideas. A famous work on community as a basis of anarchism was the book by the American anarchist Paul Goodman, *Communitas* (Goodman, 1960). Marxism has been one of the most influential communitarian movements, with its elevation of the collective interests of the community above those of the individual (Kamenka, 1982b). Many Marxists saw socialism as anticipated by the Christian millenarian movements. For Marx, the Paris Commune of 1871 was a demonstration of the promise of political community in a radical and egalitarian form. Unlike many other socialists and anarchists, Marx did not idealize the community of the past, rooted in tradition, guilds and/or in ways of life. His conception of community was urban, egalitarian and universalistic. In contrast, the anarchist Proudhon saw community in terms of small-scale local groupings.

It is possible to summarize the main conceptions of community as a normative ideal that emerged in the nineteenth century in terms of three discourses:

1   *The discourse of community as irretrievable*. This is the discourse of romantic but conservatively inclined critiques of modernity. One of its main expressions is nostalgia. On the whole this is an anti-modernist ideology.

2   *The discourse of community as recoverable*. This has been the main discourse of modern conservatism as it emerged in the early nineteenth century. Conservative thought has stood for the recovery of tradition and an organic unity of state and society. The communitarian ideal typifies conservativism, which may

be understood as an attempt to reconcile community to the conditions of modernity. Another major example of this is nationalism. The idea of political community in nationalism is necessarily tied to a primordial cultural community. The nation, embodied in the political form of the state, has generally been held to express a cultural or civic community, as shaped by a common history, language, customs and so on. In a different form republicanism has stood for a conception of community as recoverable from the past. The republican idea has generally been conceived in terms of the classical ideal of the self-governing civic community. For Alexis de Tocqueville in his famous book *Democracy in America* (1969) 2 vols, 1835 and 1840, America represented the true political community and where European civilization was redeemed. In this interpretation, America is a society in which the state does not exist outside the civic community.

3   *The discourse of community as yet to be achieved.* This is the more explicitly utopian ideal of community as expressed in the discourses of communism, socialism and anarchism where community is an ideal to be achieved, rather than being simply recovered from the past. The most influential exponent of community in this utopian sense has been Karl Marx. In Marxism the state is a political form that represents the alienation of the social dimension. Society itself can realize human potentialities only through the abolition of capitalism and its political form, the bourgeois state. The communist society is a pure society without a state.

Of the major political ideologies of modernity liberalism is the only one that is not constructed around the communitarian ideal. Because of its belief in individualism, liberalism has been sceptical of the promises of community. Although classical liberalism has looked to the more pragmatic idea of happiness as an aspiration, a perfect political community for liberalism is not possible and may even be undesirable.

THE TOTAL COMMUNITY

The twentieth-century experience of community has been one of extremes. The utopian visions of community inherited from the Enlightenment gave way to anti-utopias as well as to new kinds of utopias that sought to overcome modernity itself. In his *Quest for Community*, Robert Nisbet (1953) uses the term 'total community' to describe the emergence of totalitarian ideologies, such as fascism and extreme forms of nationalism. The total community is a community that is a fusion of state and society, an organic whole. The totalitarian state achieved a total identification of society by the state, in effect obliterating the social.

According to George Mosse (1982) the radical right took over the communal idea in the final decades of the nineteenth century. Until then it had been a radical left ideal, subversive of the status quo and offering a vision of a more egalitarian and democratic society. But, with the waning of the Enlightenment ideas and the rise of chauvinistic and authoritarian kinds of nationalism, the quest for community became more and more part of a right-wing political current. Gustav Le Bon's *The Crowd*, published in 1895, influenced the radical right, including Hitler and Mussolini, who both read it (Le Bon, 1995). In the age of mass politics, the idea of community could be invoked to express the national community, with its emphasis on exclusivity and pristine and masculine primordiality. The crowd, the *Volk*, the primordial community became much the same in the nascent new right movements of the first decades of the twentieth century. With its stress on the closely knit male community, camaraderie and youthful vigour, the German youth movement, the *Bund*, expressed this spiritual longing for community. Like the revolutionary idea of community it was also subversive of the status quo, and also of the rising tide of the movement for women's emancipation, which was relatively advanced in Germany. This combination, along with the re-mythologization of history, created a reactionary political philosophy based on a primordial community. Fascism was the ultimate expression of this kind of symbolic and sacred community, which provided a legitimation of authoritarian politics based on elites, racism and the aesthetization of politics. 'In the end,' wrote George Mosse, 'the radical right had compounded, not solved the problem of community in the modern age' (Mosse, 1982, p. 42).

These themes were central to an important work on community by the German philosopher Helmut Plessner, who claimed that the idea of community is a dangerous one. In a neglected work published in 1924, but not translated into English until 1999, *The Limits of Community*, Plessner presented a major critique of the idea of community from the standpoint of his philosophical anthropology. Rejecting the anti-modern position associated with Martin Heidegger and the nascent communitarian spirit in German thought, he claimed community was an overvalued ideal and contained a latent authoritarianism. 'The idol of this age is community' and is being directed to the 'weak of the world', he complained in this work, the aim of which was to defend modern society against the spectre of community (Plessner, 1999, pp. 66–7).

The twentieth century has been the 'age of extremes', according to Hobsbawm (1994) in the well-known book of that title. In the present context this is witnessed by alternative communal movements that are opposed to modernity and to universalistic conceptions of community. The Kibbutz is the best example of a communal movement that embodies a vision of a total community that also reflects an alternative to modernity. Rather than being another modernity, the Kibbutz movement is an alternative modernity in the sense of being a retreat from modern society and based on a particular conception of community. Erik Cohen writes that it appealed to the 'postmodern youth and intellectuals as an exemplary form of alternative communal living' (Cohen, 1982, p. 123). However, the kind of community it gave expression to was also flexible, capable of change and adaptation and never taking one immutable form. In this it differed from authoritarian kinds of total community. Moreover, of course, the Kibbutz was a voluntary community and one that was organizationally reflexive. A product of modernity, it none the less offered a different model of social relations and political organization to the frameworks that emerged in the modern age. Based on co-operation, collective ownership, equality, consensual values and secular self-government, the Kibbutz gave expression to a kind of total community. This kind of community was essentially the vision of a society without a state, for one of its chief characteristics was the absence of a state. In this sense it was one of the closest realizations of Marx's communist society. A contrast to the other kinds of total community that characterized the twentieth century, which reduced the society to the state, the Kibbutz movement reduced the domain of the state to the level of the social.

But how representative was the Kibbutz movement of community? In many ways it was an exception. Perhaps because it was a total community, possessing the elements neither of the wider society nor of the state, and being defined by its rejection of the values of the modern world, the Kibbutz movement differed from other kinds of community, whether rural or urban. Viewed in the wider perspective of history, it becomes more significant. Since the Renaissance and the Reformation, there have been many experiments in total community. Some famous conceptions of utopia in this period were Thomas More's *Utopia* [1516], Tommaso Campanella's *City of the Sun* [1623], Francis Bacon's *New Atlantis* [1629] and James Harrington's *Oceana* [1675]. Under the influence of the early utopias of the Renaissance period and the revolutionary upheavals of the early modern period, communal movements seeking an alternative to western civilizations became established. During the English Revolution when radical puritanism was on the rise, many radical movements surfaced such as the Seekers, the Diggers, the Ranters and the Levellers. Several of these established alternative communities, which Christopher Hill has compared to communism (Hill, 1975; see also Armytage, 1961). The persecution of the Puritan sects in the reformation period led to the flight of several groups to North America. The Amish community is one of the most well known of these total commmunities in North America. The Amish Mennonites, who fled to the USA from the early eighteenth century, represent one of the most enduring expressions of community as a total phenomenon. But non-conformism was the overriding feature of communal life in these communities and as such they were communities formed in opposition to modernity.

This all leads to the question whether community is a kind of terror, destroying the most social characteristics of human societies, such as their capacity for creative renewal and concern with human autonomy. Experiments in total community leave no room for individuality and creativity, even though, paradoxically, such communal movements are products of human design even when they claim to be rooted in an ancient past. They cannot be called traditional, since they are in fact products of modernity, and they have not survived without considerable effort and dedication to an ideal. In this they differ from the kinds of community to be discussed in Chapter 2, where the encounter of tradition and modernity is decisive. The total community is a regulated moral totality that is a creation of human design rather than being the product of tradition. Of course tradition can be made, and the endurance of the community over time, in the case of the Amish community over several centuries, does in the end amount to tradition. In the case of these total communities, the role of tradition is only one aspect of their self-legitimation. Another aspect is the belief in the radical otherness of the movement. Rejection of the modern world and the conscious search for a radical alternative has been central to the identity of many communal movements based on total community. An example of this is the early monastic orders. When these were founded in the early Middle Ages, the millenarian ideal of early Christianity led to a rejection of the existing and imperfect social world and the quest for an ideal world. But, as Weber pointed out in his theory of the paradox of societal rationalization, the monastic orders ultimately rationalized the social world by cultivating a new and 'disenchanted' cultural ethos in which the sacred was gradually brought closer to the profane.

CONCLUSION

In this chapter community was looked at through the lens of history and political thought. It was argued that some of the most influential conceptions of community in history have been primarily about community as a normative ideal, either as something particular or as a universal concept. In either case these quests were deeply transformative of the status quo. Community is far from being conservative and affirmative. While many of the programmatic ideologies of the post-Enlightenment period, the Age of Ideology, have reflected the universalistic conception of community, other visions of community – such as the radical communal movements of the Amish community and the Kibbutzim – have reflected a more particular conception of community. Our whole understanding of community has been influenced by these two stands. In addition, it was also emphasized strongly that the discourse of community has been dominated by a narrative of loss and recovery. An influential view is that modernity destroys community which must be recovered and realized in a new form. As argued in this chapter, this form has been mostly a political one. In Chapter 2 we turn to the sociological and anthropological interpretation of community as a social and cultural entity. In these accounts of community, what is stressed is the fluid nature of community as an expression of modalities of belonging. Rather than see community as something spatially fixed and corresponding to a particular kind of social arrangement, the suggestion here is to see community as an expression of *communitas*; that is, a particular mode of imagining and experiencing social belonging as a communicative, public happening. No social arrangement has ever fully realized *communitas* or can do without it.

Before proceeding further there is one final observation to make about the major historical accounts of community. In the classical conceptions of community the communicative nature of community was rarely discussed, with one major exception: namely Immanuel Kant. Kant anticipated the ideas of a later modernity in advocating a quasi-communicative theory of community. In *The Critique of Judgement*, published in 1790, Kant outlined the idea of a 'sensus communis' in order to explain the universality of aesthetic taste:

> by the name *sensus communis* is to be understood the idea of *public* sense, i.e. a critical faculty which in its reflective act takes account (*a priori*) of the mode of representation of every one else, in order, *as it were*, to weigh its judgement with the collective judgement of mankind, and thereby avoid the illusion arising from subjective and personal conditions which could readily be taken for objective, an illusion that would exert a prejudicial influence upon its judgement.
>
> (Kant, 1952, p. 151)

Kant goes on to argue that 'when civilization has reached its height it makes this work of communication almost the main business of refined inclination, and the entire value of sensations is placed in the degree that they permit of universal communication' (p. 156). Kant's notion of communication was limited, but it offered the first major conception of community as a process of communication, as opposed to a symbolic, institutional or purely normative ideal. The communicative dimension of community will be discussed in later chapters.

2

COMMUNITY AND SOCIETY
Myths of modernity

From the late nineteenth century a new debate about community emerged. With the rise of sociology and anthropology, community began to be conceived in terms of cultural community rather than a political ideal. The classical conceptions of community were discussed in Chapter 1. It was argued that for much of the modern age community signified a normative conception of society – an ideal to be attained. Community was defined in opposition to the state rather than to society. The twentieth century was to bring about a change in the understanding of society and with this went a corresponding change in the idea of community. Community became perceived as based more and more on the allegedly 'thick' values of tradition, a moral entity on the one side and, on the other, society became increasingly an alien and objective entity and based on very 'thin' values. In this dichotomy, the very idea and reality of *communitas* as a form of imagining social relations disappeared or was diluted. As the distinction between society and the state became less evident, community came to be seen as the residual category of social, namely that which is left when society becomes more and more rationalized by the state and by economic relations.

The interest in community as an alternative to society was clearly a consequence of the mood of crisis that came with the twentieth century, which, in contrast to the previous century, was a century of unending crisis. After a long period of peace following the Napoleonic wars, the twentieth century began with a mood of war. Beginning with the Franco-Prussian war and culminating with the First World War, modernity entered its first major crisis. One expression of this was the idea of the malaise of the social. The legitimating myth of community as a normative foundation of modern society disintegrated. From Nietzsche to Freud, intellectuals and writers began to portray modern society as being in the throes of a malaise. In classical sociology, this tendency is captured by Max Weber's metaphor of the 'iron cage', Durkheim's concern with suicide and the motif of 'anomie', and Simmel's theory of the 'tragedy of culture'. As the European nations prepared for war, the nation-state, the effective expression of modern society as a territorial phenom- enon, had become a war machine. That neither society nor state was founded on a principle of community became altogether clear. The malaise of society led to a new and essentially sociological interest in community either as an alternative to modernity or as the real basis of social integration.

The polarity of society versus community may also be seen as an expression of the essentially Protestant view of modernity. As is suggested by the work of Max Weber, the ethos cultivated by Protestantism was one that reserved meaning and spirituality for the inner world, seeing in the outer world of the social the signs of degeneration and meaninglessness. The idea of community was undoubtedly fostered more by this Protestant sensibility than by the Roman Catholic view of modernity in which institutions would play a greater role. The Protestant emphasis on an inner realm of spirituality and meaning was mirrored in the growing disenchantment with society and the turn to community as a more meaningful realm that came with modernity. Community thus came to be seen as the natural habitus of the individual and society an alien and essentially meaningless world. There is then a certain parallel in the relation of society to community and in the relation of church to sect, a distinction made by the classical sociologists Max Weber and Ernst Troeltsch. The sect designates the breakaway by a group from the rigid, institutional church which is no longer able to sustain a spirit of belonging. In much the same way we see community as a retreat from the wider society and social institutions.

In this chapter we look at the debate about community and society as it developed in modern sociology and anthropology. In essence this debate revolves around the question of whether community is a form of tradition and therefore at odds with modernity which is post-traditional. The general argument put forward in this chapter is that in fact modernity produces tradition – in the sense of inventing new traditions – and at the same time rests on the traditions inherited from the past, which are far from alien to modern society. Moreover, tradition is not pristine and primordial. Premodern societies were not based on primordial communities any more than modern societies have eradicated community. In this view, then, community and society are not fundamentally opposed but mutual forms of sociability. The assumption underlying this thesis is that community is not to be understood exclusively in terms of tradition but entails particular forms of symbolically constituted social relationships which can also be mobilized under the conditions of modernity and which are always present in every social arrangement. Drawing on some of the major sociological theories of community, it is argued that community can take post-traditional as well as traditional forms.

In the following sections, three major debates on community are critically examined. First, the notion of community as tradition, especially with regard to Tönnies. Second, the idea of moral community, especially around the work of Durkheim. Third, the theory of symbolic community, as proposed originally by Victor Turner and recently restated by Anthony Cohen. The general conclusion of this chapter is that community must be understood as an expression of a highly fluid *communitas* – a mode of belonging that is symbolic and communicative – rather than an actual institutional arrangement, and that it is variable, capable of sustaining modern and radical social relationships as well as traditional ones.

COMMUNITY AS TRADITION

The equation of community with tradition and more generally with a premodern world that began to be lost with modernity was implicit in much of modern sociology, which inherited neo-romantic ideas. One of the dominating themes in early sociology was the idea of an epochal shift from tradition to modernity. Modernity was seen as having eroded tradition, replacing it with the world of formal and rationalized structures of mass society. Henry Summer Maine, in an influential work *Ancient Law*, in 1861 presented a picture of the transition from a world based on status to one based on contract (Maine, 1905). In another work first published in 1871, *Village Communities in the East and West*, community is associated with a spatial category (Maine, 1895).[1] Accounts such as these cultivated the modern sociological idea of community as a primordial and integrative world that fades with the coming of modernity. This dichotomy was reflected in the distinction between culture and civilization that was particularly popular in Germany from the late nineteenth century onwards. Civilization – as the material expression of culture – was seen as in decline and a motif of the decadence of modernity more generally. Culture in contrast to civilization – which in German has a lower value than *Kultur* – was more spiritual and the container of values. It was inevitable that this distinction became associated with the distinction between society and community. Community suggested deeper cultural values, which were destroyed by the *Gesellschaft* of a civilization in decline.

The most famous work on community as traditional cultural values is Ferdinand Tönnies' *Community and Society*, originally published in German in 1887 as *Gemeinschaft und Gesellschaft* (Tönnies, 1963). The argument is too well known to warrant detailed explication, but a few points need to be made since, as with many works that have attained the status of a classic, it may be interpreted in many ways and virtually every study on community has defined itself in relation to this book. One of the main problems is that the German terms *Gemeinschaft* and *Gesellschaft* do not translate easily into the terms 'community' and 'society'. The German term *Gemeinschaft* indicates a sense of community that incorporates certain elements of associative life. It is not purely a matter of traditional or hierarchical social relations based on face-to-face relations. While there is no doubt that Tönnies tended to polarize these terms, seeing community as encompassing tradition and society as modernity, and both interlocked in a 'tragic conflict' (p. 162), it is evident from the first page of this work that he saw these as two kinds of associative life.[2] Unfortunately too many textbooks on classical sociology have failed to note this important point. At the beginning of the work, Tönnies argues that community and society are different expressions of social relationships and which can be understood as products of human wills. 'The relationship itself, and also the resulting association, is conceived of either as real and organic life – this is the essential characteristic of the Gemeinschaft (community); or as imaginary and mechanical structure – this is the concept of Gesellschaft (society)' (p. 33). Towards the end of the book, he writes, 'the essence of both Gemeinschaft and

Gesellschaft is found interwoven in all kinds of associations' (p. 249). His argument is that with modernity, society replaces community as the primary focus for social relations. Community is 'living', while society is mechanical. The former is more rooted in locality and is 'natural', while the latter is more a 'rational', 'mental' product and one that is sustained by relations of exchange.

Community as *Gemeinschaft* is expressed, to follow Tönnies' terms, in family life in concord, in rural village life in folkways, and in town life in religion. Society as *Gesellschaft* is expressed in city life in convention, in national life in legislation, and in cosmopolitan life in public opinion (see p. 231). These are the terms Tönnies uses and which indicate that community and society, while being very different, express different kinds of associative life. In the ensuing discussion, which reflects an evolutionary view of society, it becomes evident that he saw the principles of society becoming progressively established in communal life, transforming it under the forces of modernity into something quite alien to community. Tönnies followed Marx in seeing the history of modern society in terms of a fundamental conflict between town and country, and in seeing the history of human society as one leading towards socialism, which 'is inherent in the concept Gesellschaft', he claimed (p. 234). The modern debate about community came to be shaped by the conflict of town and countryside, which came to replace the earlier dichotomy of society and the state.

Although Tönnies has been seen as a romantic conservative, looking backwards at the lost world of the traditional rural community, in fact he was an ardent socialist and lost his professorial chair for supporting strike action in Hamburg in the 1890s. Inspired by French utopian socialism, and the work of Lorenz Stein in particular, he supported traditional forms of socialism, such as guild socialism, as well as more radical kinds of socialism and various kinds of reformism. In fact he held that socialism was as natural to society as individualism. Thus in view of his political position we get a more differentiated analysis of his famous book. *Community and Society* is not at all like Edmund Burke's *Reflections on the Revolution in France* [1790], a reactionary eulogy to traditional and feudal society, but an attempt to outline 'basic sociological concepts', as the German subtitle announces, and to offer a critique of 'bourgeois society'. Tönnies was not always nostalgic about the passing of community, which he did not think could resist capitalist modernity without a political will. In correcting the conventional interpretation of Tönnies, however, it must be pointed out that his theory of modern society was constrained by a narrow evolutionary view of modernity replacing tradition and with it community. He saw community as a product of 'natural wills', while society is the creation of 'rational wills' which leaves little room for the former. This view of modernity, which was heavily influenced by neo-romanticism, failed to appreciate how tradition is produced by modernity, and that much of our view of tradition is a product of modernity.

Since Tönnies, modern sociology became greatly preoccupied with the problem of the survival of community in modernity. Robert Redfield's (1955) *The Little Community* is a good example of the sociological literature that emerged with the rise of sociology as an academic discipline.[3] Although urban sociology was to put community on a different level, much of the early sociology of community was based on anthropological studies of traditional peasant communities, with many of these being inspired by Evans-Pritchard's famous study of the Nuer (Evans-Pritchard, 1940). The Nuer lived in communities not in societies and there was no sense of a wider society. The community encompassed the social and the cultural in classical anthropology. This conflation of the social and the cultural in the anthropological concept of community, which saw primitive societies as holistic cultures, suggested a model of community that more or less expressed the sociological idea of tradition. Communities for modern sociology survive in modernity as fairly cohesive entities and are resistant to modern society.

This approach is exemplified in the studies of Arensberg and Kimball; for instance, their classic work *Family and Community in Ireland* (Arensberg and Kimball, 1940/1968).[4] The idea of community in this famous work in positivistic ethnology was never actually defined but the underlying assumption was that of the moral force deposited in the customary and long-term relations of rural traditions. Community is not a symbolically constructed reality but a 'master system' of relationships that exists beyond and above its members. A certain determinism lay behind a view of community as an ordered whole regulated by highly structured relationships concerning the familistic order, age, sex, work and trade. As mentioned above, some notion of primitive communalism often lay behind the myth of the traditional community, which rarely questioned the idea of tradition, believing it to be an unchanging order, whereas in fact many traditions are products of modernization. The rural community in southern Ireland examined by Arensberg and Kimball in the late 1930s was itself the product of social and economic modernization that began in the previous century but which has now long vanished from Irish society.[5] It was far from the timeless community that is suggested by their work. In fact the alleged 'traditional' community was a product of rapid modernization in rural Ireland which experienced major social and economic change in the nineteenth century. The family and kinship structures examined by Arensberg and Kimball were probably no older than a few generations.

What emerges from such studies is a view of culture as integrative and total. While today culture is largely seen as a site of conflict, in this pre-multicultural era of classical anthropology and sociology, culture was a force of stability and integration akin to tradition. This view of culture as holistic was given systematic attention in Parsons' structural functionalism. Community and culture had in common the function of maintaining social integration.[6] For Parsons: 'A community is that collectivity the members of which share a common territorial area as that base of operations for daily activities' (Parsons, 1951, p. 91; see also Parsons, 1960). But for Parsons, community was possible in modernity and was the basis of social integration even in the most functionally differentiated societies. The 'societal community' ultimately underpinned the social system and guaranteed the essential unity of society (Parsons, 1961, p. 10). The concept of the societal community in Parsons' work is at best vague, indicating the integrative function of the social system.[7] In a more specific usage, community was one of the four types of social groups, the others being kinship, ethnicity and class (Parsons, 1951, p. 173). However, at this point we have to go beyond the idea of community as tradition, since the Durkheimean heritage that Parsons drew from emphasized community less in terms of tradition than in terms of morality. Modern community is differentiated from traditional community in being a civic community.

COMMUNITY AS A MORAL FORCE

We now move slowly to a post-traditional understanding of community. Tönnies' notion of community was almost entirely one that equated community with tradition, seeing society as being composed of different kinds of social relations. Durkheim in contrast held to a different understanding of community. In fact he was very critical of Tönnies. In a review of *Community and Society* in 1889 he disagreed with Tönnies' notion of *Gesellschaft*, or society. Accepting Tönnies' argument that society derives from community, he argued that society is not primarily characterized by a utilitarian individualism and mechanical social relations. In Durkheim's view, life in large groups is as natural as in small ones, claiming 'there is a collective activity in our contemporary societies which is just as natural as that of the smaller societies of previous ages' (Durkheim, 1964, pp. 146–7). Durkheim rejected the assumption that lay behind Tönnies' argument of community as organic and society as mechanical. In fact in his major work on modern society, *The Division of Labour in Society*, first published in 1893, he effectively reversed Tönnies' thesis, claiming that in fact in modernity organic forms of solidarity are emerging and replacing the mechanical forms of the past. Moreover, he disagreed with Tönnies' view that only the state can reverse the destructive impact of the individualism that comes with modern society. For Durkheim only civic forms of solidarity based on citizenship can do this (Durkheim, 1957). The problem with Tönnies' sociology for Durkheim was that it ignored the very real forms of community that came with modernity. Moreover, he rejects the view that individualism, interest and diversity are necessarily bad. The question for Durkheim rather was what kind of moral order is best able to deal with the problems of the modern age.

Underlying Durkheim's sociology was a notion of community that was specific to modernity and which may be understood as a form of moral individualism. His entire sociology was an attempt to find an answer to the question of what kind of social integration can exist in modern society. It may be suggested that the concept of community with which he was primarily concerned is post-traditional community, namely forms of solidarity that are specific to modernity. Such a view challenges the old picture of Durkheim as an opponent of modernization and a defender of collective morality. Although this view never gained widespread currency in Europe, classical American sociology generally regarded Durkheim as antithetical to American individualism. While Parsons helped to correct this view, as did Jeffrey Alexander more recently, the bias persisted, as is evident from the repre-sentation of his thought by such sociologists as Robert Nisbet, Alvin Gouldner and Lewis Coser for whom the very idea of functionalism, with which Durkheim was associated, indicated an affirmative attitude. However, in recent interpretations of his thought, he is portrayed much more unequivocally as a communitarian defender of liberalism (see Cladis, 1992; Stedman Jones, 2001). Central to this is his view of moral individualism as the basis of a new kind of civic morality that might be capable of combating egoistic individualism. What liberalism needs is more of the former, but Durkheim believed that the basic norms of moral individualism are already to be found in organic forms of solidarity that are emerging with the division of labour in society. Organic solidarity is a contrast to mechanical solidarity in that it is based on co-operation, pluralism and a certain individualism. The glue that held modern society together was a civic morality articulated in citizenship and above all in education, Durkheim argued. Solidarity in modern society is not mechanical but organic in the sense that it is a means of achieving integration within the context of societal differentiation and the formation of ever larger social frameworks. These larger and more differentiated societies can function only if they achieve a different kind of solidarity. In traditional societies integration is more mechanical in the sense that there is less space for the autonomy of groups and individuals who mechanically reproduce the collective norms and values of society. Organic solidarity is the basis for a new kind of community and which is expressed in more abstract kinds of 'collective representation'. In earlier societies these were largely defined by religion, but in modern society they are more abstract and plural due to societal differentiation. The malaise of modern society for Durkheim was not the collapse of the older collective representations but the failure of modernity to evolve a new spirit of community which might be called post-traditional. The phenomenon of suicide, the anti-Semitism epitomized by the Dreyfus Affair, the extreme nationalism of the early twentieth century can be cited as examples of the pathological consequences of the absence of an appropriate form of community in modern society which consequently falls back on older forms of community but ones which are not adequate for the demands of modernity.

The argument presented here, then, is that a second and major strand in modern sociology, best represented by Durkheim, regards community as post-traditional. In this view, and in contrast to the myth of traditional community, the emphasis is on community as a moral force and which is essentially civic in nature. The role of tradition is relatively unimportant. Max Weber also defined community in a way that left it open to tradition or post-traditional possibilities: 'A social relationship will be called "communal" in and so far as the orientation of social action – whether in the individual case, on the average, or in the pure type – is based on a subjective feeling of the parties, whether affectual or traditional, that they belong together' (Weber, 1947, p. 136). In contrast, an associative relationship, Weber says, 'rests on a rationally motivated adjustment of interests or a similarly motivated agreement, whether the basis of rational judgement be absolute values or reasons of expediency' (ibid.). Weber also points out that while conflict is more typically absent from communal relationships, this should not 'be allowed to obscure the fact that coercion of all sorts is a very common thing in even the most intimate of such communal relationships if one party is weaker than the other' (p. 137). However, Weber tended to discount the possibility of community emerging under the rationalized conditions of modernity.

In one of the most important works on community in later German sociology, *The Community*, René König criticizes the view that only in small-scale rural society can there be integration while in the town there is only social disorganization. 'In fact, an unprejudiced approach shows that even a small community can be structurally so differentiated that formidable obstacles are placed in the way of integration – no less in small communities than in large' (König, 1968, p. 196). His view of community was not too distant from that of Durkheim in that he believed community was a primary source of strength for all kinds of societies and that there are different kinds of community. Thus the difference between the present and the past is not the passing of community but the coming into being of a new kind of community. His definition of community as 'a global society on a local basis' has resonances in recent studies on globalization. According to König, the distinctive feature of community is a certain consciousness of the mutual connections between people. Thus it is not important how big or small it is or whether it is an administrative unit, as in the German word for associative communities, the *Gemeinde*, or traditional or modern, rural or urban. Joseph Gusfield makes a similar point when he says: 'rather than conceiving of "community" and "society" as groups and/or entities to which persons "belong", it would seem more useful to conceptualize these terms as points of reference brought into play in particular situations and arenas' (Gusfield, 1975, p. 41).

That community may be possible in a post-traditional world has been a theme running through much of British sociology. Raymond Williams looked to a modern kind of community based on solidarity and equality as opposed to traditional rural values. In his major work *Culture and Society*, culture is not the site of integrative, consensual pristine values but a product of modern society (Williams, 1961). As communities become transformed by modernity, there is a decline of traditional community but not always the emergence of a new kind of community. In a classic study of modern urban communities, *Tradition and Change: A Study of Banbury*, the sociologist Margaret Stacey concluded:

> It is even doubtful whether there is a sense of community among all of those who were born and brought up in the town. For those who are still part of the traditional small-town society, who own, manage, or work in its traditionist shops and smaller factories,

who provide the traditional services, who belong to the close-knit
and long-standing groups in clubs and pubs and who accept
the traditional standards, there is certainly some sense of
community, some feeling of belonging. This is expressed through
loyalty to the town and its established institutions. Groups of
immigrants who shared together the experiences of coming to
the town and settling down there and especially those who live
as neighbours have a sense of belonging to a group within the
town and not the town itself.

(Stacey, 1960, p.177)

This questioning of community as a holistic entity is also present
in Robert Moore's studies on Durham mining communities. He
showed that working-class communities are not traditional and,
more importantly, tradition takes numerous forms, with religious
traditions and trade union association producing different
allegiances (Moore, 1974). In another study of Peterhead in
Scotland, Moore demonstrated that despite all the appearances
of homogeneity, there were major divisions in the community
where self-interest prevailed as much as solidarity or ties of
belonging (Moore, 1982).

Community in general concerns particular forms of belonging
and the decline of community can be a decline only in particular
ties of belonging, which must be measured by the rise of
other forms of belonging. This question regarding the communal
forms of belonging in urban society was one of the chief concerns
of the early Chicago School and dominated much of American
urban sociology (see Chapter 3). The new disciplines of urban
sociology and community studies sought answers to the question
of what kind of community is possible in modern urban
contexts.[8] This is one way of relativizing the false dualism of
society/community and tradition/modernity.

In a study of the 'radicalness of tradition' Craig Calhoun
indicates another route to conceiving the relation of tradition and

community. He has argued that traditional communities have been important bases of collective mobilization. Such communities have possessed the necessary associative structures to resist the disruptive effects of modernization. He stresses the multidimensional nature of community in terms of autonomous control, social relationship, social networks which can be mobilized for collective action. Many peasant revolts in nineteenth-century Europe were based on communal forms of organization, which is something that Marx never recognized. Thus rather than seeing a radical break with socialism, Calhoun argues for a continuity between the corporatism of the past and modern socialism. Traditional communities provide important structures for shared interests and a capacity for collective action to develop (Calhoun, 1982, 1983). 'Traditional communities are important bases of radical mobilization. Community constitutes the preexisting organization capable of securing the participation of individuals in collective action. Communities provide a social organizational foundation for mobilization, as networks of kinship, friendship, shared crafts, or recreations offer lines of communication and allegiance' (Calhoun, 1983, p. 897). In particular in England, Calhoun argues that their members worked in fairly modern capitalist contexts and were not committed to an unchanging lifestyle based on traditional, preindustrial values. For Calhoun, what is distinctive about these traditional communities in nineteenth-century Europe was not the binding force of traditional values as such, but collective resources and a capacity for collective action.

The assumption that modern social relations are absent from traditional community has been criticized heavily in a recent volume on community in India. Several critics have pointed out that the Gandhian notion of Indian village life was derived largely from colonial/orientalist writings (Jodhka, 2002). Carol Upadhya (2002, p. 36) argues against orthodox interpretations, such as Louis Dummont, that underlying the debate about community is a dichotomy of culture and economy, with culture being associated with religion, caste and community and which is destroyed by economic forces, such as class. This is present in a false understanding of the 'jajmani system' as a non-monetary system for the exchange of goods and services within a village community and differing from the western rational, self-seeking individual. Her approach is to demonstrate that community is not a clearly defined, homogeneous kind of social grouping separate from class and other dimensions of social interaction and, moreover, it is characterized by conflict, oppression, exploitation and patriarchy. This thesis also takes issue with the primacy of community in postcolonial writings.

Finally, within the classical tradition, it is important to note another conception of community which departs from the community/society dualism. Herman Schmalenbach drew attention to the rise of small groups in modern society, the associative and communal *Bünde*, such as the *Freundschaftsbünde* (friendship associations or clubs) (Schmalenbach, 1977). In a work written in 1922 Schmalenbach suggested that the traditional community as described by Tönnies is based largely on involuntary ties in that its members are born into it. Society is different, requiring more conscious effort and rational forms of action. What he drew attention to is the role of group-based organization in modern society which, while being entered into voluntarily and thus requiring conscious action, also reflects some characteristics of community, for instance, in strong ties of obligation and co-operation. He was highly critical of Tönnies' theory of community. 'The term, community,' he wrote, 'has become a catchword used to designate every possible (as well as the most impossible) delusion of the time' (Schmalenbach, 1977, p. 64). He distinguished the phenomenon of 'communion' as a sociological category distinct from community and society to indicate emotional experiences, such as those of the crowd. In modern society, as Georg Simmel also recognized, these small group or *bünde*-like communities would become more and more important. Indeed, as he argued, small groups can be as complex in the organization as large ones. This approach to community as communion is also reflected in Victor Turner's concept of *communitas* as a spontaneous, communal emotion, akin to Durkheim's 'creative effervescence', an idea he adopted.[9] This will now be considered in more detail.

SYMBOLIC COMMUNITY AND LIMINALITY

Victor Turner's seminal work *The Ritual Process: Structure and Anti-Structure* reoriented the anthropological study of community (Turner, 1969). The book is famous primarily for its celebrated discussion of liminality, a concept borrowed from an earlier work by Arnold Van Gennep (1960), and which has resonances in recent postmodernist writing. Liminality refers to those 'between' moments, such as carnivals, pilgrimages, rites of passage or rituals in which normality is suspended. Liminality – 'moments in and out of time' – is thus often connected with those moments of symbolic renewal when a society or group asserts its collective identity. Although these moments can become highly institutionalized – as in church rites – they are expressive of creativity and perform important social functions. In the present context what is particularly interesting is that Turner discusses liminality not in exclusively symbolic terms but as an expression of what he calls 'communitas'; while not being the only expression of liminality, it is one of the most significant.

According to Victor Turner community is best understood as communitas to distinguish a particular kind of social relationship that exists in all kinds of society and which is not reducible to community in the sense of a fixed and spatially specific grouping. He makes a sharp distinction between communitas and primitive or archaic society, seeing communitas as present in all kinds of society (Turner, 1969, pp. 96, 130). Communitas is sustained by 'anti-structure', when 'structures' are resisted. It emerges when anti-structures come into play. Liminal moments are particularly important expressions of anti-structure, as in, for instance, counter-cultural currents: 'In modern Western society, the values of communitas are strikingly present in the literature and behaviour of what came to be known as the "beat generation", who were succeeded by the "hippies", who, in turn, have a junior division known as the "teeny-boppers"' (Turner, 1969, p. 112).

Turner's argument about community is that community is to be understood in opposition to structure. It is not something characteristic of premodern societies, nor is it anti-modern nor the antithesis to society. While defined against the norm-governed, institutionalized and abstract nature of social structure, communitas is the expression of the social nature of society. 'Communitas breaks in through the interstices of structure, in liminality; at the edges of structure, in marginality; and from beneath structure, in inferiority' (Turner, 1969, p. 128). For Turner, communitas has a cognitive as well as a symbolic role to play:

> Liminality, marginality, and structural inferiority are conditions in which are frequently, symbols, rituals, philosophical systems, and works of art. These cultural forms provide men with a set of templates or models which are, at one level, periodical reclassi-fications of reality and man's relationship to society, nature, and culture. But they are more than classifications, since they incite men to action as well as to thought.
>
> (Turner, 1969, pp. 128–9)

Underlying his theory of communitas is a view of social relationships – the *We* – as transient and liminal. Community as sponteanous communitas is 'always unique, and hence socially transient'. But there are also the forms, such as normative com-munitas and ideological communitas, which unlike spontaneous communitas are within the limits of structure. This differentiated account of communitas offers an important corrective to reductive accounts of community and moreover has the merit in drawing attention to the creative role of community in shaping different forms of social relations. It suggests a view of community as an anti-structural moment *within* society.

For Turner community has a symbolic character in the sense here of creating powerful links between members of a society or social group. His theory stressed the binding nature of communitas. Anthony Cohen, in an important book *The Symbolic Construction of Community*, which owes much to Turner, offers a slightly different account of community. He argues that community is based on the symbolic construction of boundaries and that this can entail different interpretations as to the meaning of communitas (Cohen, 1985). Opposing all attempts to reduce community to institutional and spatial categories or historical narratives, he defines community in terms of particular kinds of awareness groups have of themselves in relation to other groups. The most significant kind of awareness is the symbolization of boundaries by which the community differentiates itself from others. Symbolization is the affirmation of the existing order of the community by boundary construction. This view of community sees it as a 'cluster of symbolic and ideological map references with which the individual is socially oriented' (Cohen, 1985, p. 57). Cohen stresses the relational aspect of community by which symbols and their enactment in rituals mark the community in relation to other communities. According to this interpretation, community exists ultimately in the symbolic order rather than in an empirical reality; it is a form of consciousness or awareness of reality; and as such community is a symbolically constructed reality. Against Turner, he argues that 'people can participate within the "same" ritual yet find quite different meanings for it' (Cohen, 1985, p. 55). This is an important point in that it shows how community is both an ideal and a kind of symbolic reality.

This interpretation of community as symbolic departs from the conventional accounts in many respects, ranging from the idea of traditional communities to the notion of moral or civic community. In both of these cases community is largely a matter of institutionalized social arrangements. The advantage of theorizing community as a symbolically constructed reality is that it avoids such reductionism. Instead community may be seen as an open system of cultural codification. In this view, symbols are cultural forms that require interpretation and their versatility is due to the fact that they are not closed systems but require interpretation. 'Symbols are effective because they are imprecise', he argues (Cohen, 1985, p. 21). While their form may persist, their content can change as society itself undergoes change. In this way, Cohen believes community can endure change while appearing to be unchanging and thus a source of stability in face of transience. Symbolization is amenable to change in many ways, including the actual form of the symbol, but most symbols can simply be interpreted in ever novel ways. Moreover, this suggests that community need not be based on uniformity: 'It is a commonality of forms (ways of behaving) whose content (meaning) may vary considerably among its members' (Cohen, 1985, p.20).

This is an important contribution to the theory of community, showing how community is not rigid but fluid and open to change. Community is not a compelling moral structure that determines behaviour but is a resource from which people may draw. However, it has two major weaknesses. It does not consider that communitas can take violent forms, where the community is sustained by violence to another group or to sub-groups within it. More generally, the debate about community as symbolic and expressed in liminal moments neglects the reality of violence in those moments of transgression. Some of the most powerful expressions of community have been disguised rites of violence. This connection of community with power and violence has been underestimated all too often in the literature. Violence is often the marker of the boundaries of a community, defining the separation of self and other. Some of the most powerful expressions of community are often experienced precisely where there has been a major injustice inflicted on a group of people, who consequently develop a sense of their common fate.

The second problem with the theory of symbolic community, as in the work of Cohen (1985) and Barth (1969) is that it stresses too much the exclusive nature of community. Communities are thus entirely shaped by the construction of boundaries and the reality of community is thus denied. But culture is more than symbolism. There are also the wider cognitive and creative aspects of culture in which social worlds are created, rather than simply affirmed. The symbolic construction of community is held generally to be that which is sustained in rituals and in the consciousness of boundaries. This is only one aspect of culture. Examples such as multiculturalism and cyberculture – and much of postmodern culture – social movements suggest a view of culture as cutting across boundaries and generally more transformative than affirmative. In contrast, however, it is the affirmative aspect of culture that is the focus in the idea of symbolic construction.

CONCLUSION

This chapter has looked at the major conceptions of community in modern sociology and anthropology, focusing in particular on the debate about community versus society. The following conclusions may be drawn from the discussion.

Community cannot be defined exclusively in terms of tradition. It has been argued that tradition in the sense of the power of the past, fixed patterns of conduct, stemming from largely preindustrial society, do not define community for the simple reason that community also exists within modernity. This leads to the argument that community can take a post-traditional form.

A second argument has been that community can take a civic and even a radical form, being very often a resource for civic association and also for more radical kinds of collective mobilization. This thesis undermines the conventional view of community as an affirmation of the status quo or as a means of achieving social integration. In other words, community can have a transformative role.

A third claim is that community and society are simply different expressions of associative structures, such as the commune, the *Gemeinde*. In this sense community is not merely a matter of traditional values but of forms of social organization and of belonging.

Fourth, it has been argued, following Victor Turner's seminal work on liminality and communitas, that one major dimension of community is that it precisely gives expression to the immediacy of the social, and is present in every kind of society as a mode of belonging and of imagining social relations.

Finally, it has been argued that community is often expressed in symbolic forms rather than being exclusively an institutional arrangement. The symbolic nature of community consists in the ability of the community to construct boundaries that are enacted in rituals. However, it was noted that culture contains more than symbols, including cognitive forms and possibilities for self-transformation. This ultimately points to a more radical conception of community.

In sum, we may say that community has been an important basis of much of modern social relationships. Community has been an important dimension of democracy, civic culture and even radicalness, and therefore cannot be defined exclusively in terms of premodern tradition.[10] Chapter 3 illustrates this more explicitly by looking at the rise of community studies and urban sociology.

3

URBAN COMMUNITY
Locality and belonging

In *The City*, Max Weber argued that the city represented one of the major achievements of western civilization (Weber, [1905] 1958). The city was the natural expression of civil society and was based on liberty and citizenship. In giving form to civic community, the city was a vibrant and dense site of inter-connecting social relations based on the autonomy of the city with respect to other political units. Weber believed the European city of the Middle Ages, especially the Hanseatic cities and other free city states, encapsulated a kind of civic community that was later to become threatened by the rationalization unleashed by modernity when the marketplace lost its ability to provide a model of integration. Absorbed into the nation-state, the city lost its autonomy, and with this came a loss of its identity. This theme of the fall of the city has been central to many interpretations of the city in modern thought, from Rousseau's praise of the ancient polis as an ideal for modern times to escape the tutelage of the state to Engels' description of Manchester in the mid-nineteenth century to Simmel's essays on the modern metropolis and T.S. Eliot's evocation of the city as a wasteland (Rousseau, [1762] 1968; Engels, [1845] 1936; Simmel, [1905] 1950; Eliot [1922] 1963). This theme of the city has been linked closely to the theme of community.

The fate of community in urban society has also been one of the main themes in modern sociology since the days of the Chicago School. This very rich sociological tradition has led to important studies on human ecology, civic design and urban regeneration which have all had human alienation as their theme. While avoiding extreme pessimism, the general theme in much of the Chicago School was one of the crisis and decline of community. However, these works did retain a basic fate in the possibility of community and, perhaps, too, a wider fate in the promise of modernization to deliver a just society. In recent years there have been signs that these concerns of the older urban sociology and community studies have been displaced by new ones, where the emphasis is more on the impact of globalization than industralization, and with postmodernization replacing modernization. In this shift in the study of community, the big question is whether cities have totally lost their connection with community, having become absorbed into the global society, and as a result the last vestiges of locality have been destroyed in the revanchivist world of the global city and its gated communities. The older sociology of the Chicago School believed the city, despite all its problems, was the natural habitat of community and represented the human order of society. This view began to be questioned by the generation of the 1960s, as in the book by Maurice Stein *The Eclipse of Community* (Stein, 1960).[1] The concerns of urban sociology moved on to other issues, such as suburbia, and urban sociology itself became overshadowed by other developments in sociology. Moreover, many of the pre-suppositions of the Chicago School, such as the basic belief in

American social institutions, the assumption that out of the urban ethnic melting-pot would rise a meritocratic society and the wider fate in universal modernization, all collapsed in the 1970s. In *The Private Future: Causes and Consequences of Community Collapse in the West* Martin Pawley summed this all up with the announcement of the decline of community in a retreat into private lives (Pawley, 1973). In recent years, however, there has been a renaissance of urban sociology, which has become linked closely with theories of globalization, social movements and new conceptions of space.

In this chapter some of these issues are explored. Beginning with the Chicago School and post-Second World War urban sociology and community studies, we move on to look at the post-Chicago School urban sociology around the work of David Harvey, Neil Smith and Mike Davis. In the third section, the work of Manuel Castells and Janet Abu-Lughod is discussed, where the focus is on the relocalization of the city by means of urban communities. The different approaches of Castells and Abu-Lughod are discussed and compared to the vision of urban degradation. We also look at some issues of urban empowerment.

THE CHICAGO SCHOOL AND AFTER

The older Chicago School – as represented by the work of Robert Park, Ernest Burgess and Louis Wirth in the 1920s, and Helen and Robert Lynd and Lloyd Warner in the 1930s – was influenced by the philosophical movement of pragmatism as associated with William James and John Dewey. It is perhaps for this reason that they were inclined to see the city as an artefact that could be fashioned by human will. Robert Park had studied under Dewey and was influenced by Dewey's strong belief in the need for greater and more pragmatic democracy which must be brought into cities and which did not need great programmatic ideologies to announce it. Thus his sociology was always connected with a pragmatic social policy, as in his well-known work, published in 1915, 'The City – Suggestions for the Investigation of Human Behaviour in the Urban Environment' (Park, 1915; see also Park, 1952).

There is little doubt that the early Chicago School saw the city through the lens of the small town or village. The American historical imagination, in contrast to the European, has been hostile to the city and this tradition of thinking may have influenced their studies on urban living as the decline of community. One tendency was to see urbanization, industrialization and modernization as transforming the town into the city, creating new kinds of social relations and presenting new challenges for community. But these sociologists were also influenced by the sociology of Georg Simmel, who emphasized the significance of small groups and established the foundations of urban sociology. This led, on the other side, to a more positive view of the city as the site of new experiences and possibilities for group formation. From Simmel, who Park introduced to American sociology, the notion arose of the city as an open structure where very different kinds of social relations and forms of belonging are possible and where human creativity may be enhanced. According to Simmel, conflict could be a basis of social integration in modern society and was not necessarily detrimental to integration as might be the case in the rural community (Simmel, 1955). Conflict can lead to a stronger identity within groups and a web or network of diverse group affiliations can be formed which does not depend on common values. This tension between the passing of the town and the arrival of the cosmopolitan city was reflected in the themes of unity and diversity. Robert Park saw the city as a mosaic of separated worlds but nevertheless capable of being co-ordinated. He believed the city might be able to achieve a certain unity based on the accommodation of diversity in what was becoming a multicultural society due to major flows of immigration.

While Park concentrated on Chicago and assumed that the patterns of urbanization there would be the norm, other urban sociologists, such as Helen and Robert Lynd in their classic study *Middletown*, looked at other towns in order to assess the impact of urbanization in the period 1890 to 1924 (Lynd and Lynd, 1929). The Lynds were struck by the collapse of the older crafts as a result of the impact of industrialization and its technical innovations. In their later work, *Middletown in Transition*, the central event of the Depression suggested a slightly different view of urban community as one under threat from major forces of societal fragmentation (Lynd and Lynd, 1937). New kinds of power are documented, the intrusion of outside forces and, with blocked mobility, the vision of arrested unity dominates this book, suggesting that the city may not be in control of its destiny. Other major works of the period (for instance, Louis Wirth's influential essay 'Urbanism as a Way of Life') described the city in terms of size, density and heterogeneity of urban communities: 'the larger, the more densely populated, and the more hetrogeneous a community, the more accentuated the characteristics associated with urbanism will be' (Wirth, 1938, p. 9). William Foote Whyte in *Street Corner Society* (Whyte, 1943) and Herbert Gans in *The Urban Villagers* (Gans, [1962] 1982) discussed the question of social cohesion and urban alienation. It would be impossible to summarize all of these works, but in the context of the present concern with the fate of urban community it might be said that these studies tended to see community as something preserved in the locality, while being under threat in the wider city.[2] An interpretation might be that the city has become absorbed into the *Gesellschaft* of society while *Gemeinschaft* is preserved in the vestiges of locality. This is evident in Herbert Gans' work and also in a study by Gerald Suttles (1968) on ethnic communities, and in Whyte's study of the Italian communities in Boston. As cities become more and more diverse and unstable due to changes in the nature of capitalism and industrialization, a sense of place and attachment, which is generally related to ethnicity, can be possible only in small localities or neighbourhoods. This of course was also the view of community in Robert Redfield's well-known book, *The Little Community*, where community is seen as small-scale, cohesive and under threat from large units (Redfield, 1955). But in the studies of urban ghettos what was stressed was the role of gangs, loyalties, local leadership and community clubs rather than the cosy world of rural America. This led to network analysis and a conception of community that stressed relationships and flows of activities, as Barry Wellman argued in an article published in 1979: 'The utility of the network perspective is that it does not take as its starting point putative solidarities – local or kin – nor does it seek primarily to find and explain the persistence of solidarity sentiments' (Wellman, 1979, p. 1203).

In effect, community was seen as pertaining to relatively small groups, such as neighbourhoods, based on mutual interdependence and common forms of life. These communities might be quite small, perhaps extending over a few blocks, but were held to be the foundation for a sense of belonging based on shared experiences, a common language, kinship ties, and above all of inhabiting a common spatial life-world. The forms of social control exercised in these neighbourhoods tended to enhance community rather than undermine it. One of the dominant themes in community and urban sociology was the defence of the community as a result of external threats to it. These studies reflected a belief in the power of local forms of urban belonging. In the urban sociology of Claude Fischer (1975, 1982, 1984) community, especially sub-cultures within the city, is seen as a means of cultural renewal for cities: 'The "subcultural theory of urbanism" holds that community size leads to a variety of distinct and intense social worlds', he wrote in direct opposition to the mainstream Chicago School (Fischer, 1982, p. 11). For him, cities are more heterogeneous than small communities, attracting migrants, and they have diverse social and professional groups. But cities do more, he argued: 'they intensify the distinctiveness of their subcultures' (1982, p. 12). Urban communities are by their size and composition self-transformative and generative of a 'pluralistic mosaic of little worlds'. This is a broadly positive view of urban community and particular kinds of social organization based on friendship and kinship networks in cities. In British sociology this approach was reflected in a long tradition of community studies, including both rural and urban communities (Bell and Newby, 1971; Moore and Rex, 1967; Young and Wilmott, 1957).

On the other side is a more disenchanted view of the city, which as already mentioned was always part of the Chicago School's approach. The city is seen as increasingly unable to deliver the promise of community conceived of as an organic urban village. The rise of suburbia and the exodus of the middle class from the city brought a new agenda to urban sociology. Transient middle-class communities inhabit these spaces, wrote William H. Whyte in *The Organization Man*, and are inhabited by the new class of 'organization men' whose allegiances lie elsewhere and where socialization is more likely to be performed by institutions such as the school than the kin (Whyte, 1957). A general trend in community studies now becomes the equation of community with social disadvantage.

THE FRAGMENTATION OF URBAN COMMUNITY: GLOBAL CITIES, GENTRIFICATION AND THE REVANCHIST CITY

The new urban sociology from the mid-1980s held an entirely different view of the city, which seemed to have exhausted the promise of modernity. Place gave way to global flows, and neighbourhoods had either become ghettos located on the 'edge city' or 'gated communities'. The restructuring of capitalism by global markets, information technology and neoliberal policies marked the end of industrialization and the coming of a new age of deindustrialization. The consequences for the city and urban communities were enormous. The city lost its connection with community.

David Harvey (1990) has been an influential critic of the 'postmodern condition'. In striking contrast to the mainstream postmodern thinkers (discussed in Chapter 7) who see something potentially liberating about postmodern community, Harvey sees only fragmentation and urban destruction. In fact, he sees postmodern community as the end of community. As an urban geographer, he is less impressed by conceptions of the postmodern condition that emphasize purely cultural and philosophical aspects of identity formation. The urban reality of American cities he claims is one of widespread polarization, homelessness, fragmentation and marginalization of urban communities. This is a position shared by other commentators on postmodernization, such as Frederic Jameson (1991), who in *Postmodernism, or, the Cultural Logic of Late Capitalism* argues that postmodernism is nothing more than the extension of capitalism into all spheres of life and consequently social struggles in the postmodern era will be fought out in the sphere of culture. Harvey has been more explicit in stressing the extension of postmodernization into the very spatial structures of society. Thus it is in the spatial structures of urban society that postmodernism is most visible, operating now as a system of social control through surveillance and fragmentation.

For Harvey there is no essential difference between post-fordist capitalism – down-sizing, flexibility, small-scale firms, offshoring, social atomization – and postmodernism which for him is a movement that replaces ethics with aesthetics and confuses atomization with autonomy. Postmodernism argues that legitimation is no longer possible and thus provides the new capitalism with what neoliberals have also been claiming, as in the phrases of the British Prime Minister Margaret Thatcher, 'there is no alternative' or 'society does not exist', for there are only markets and individual consumers. Postmodernism merely tells people to accept the reality of fragmentation and the absence of any meaningful relation to their environment, since shared values and forms of life are alleged to have died with modernity. As he puts it in the *The Condition of Postmodernity*: 'Worst of all, while it opens up a radical prospect by acknowledging the authenticity of other voices, postmodernist thinking immediately shuts off those other voices from access to more universal sources of power by ghettoizing them within an opaque otherness, the specificity of this or that language game' (Harvey, 1990, p. 117). While he accepts that some aspects of postmodernism have been important in highlighting difference, this has been at the cost of ignoring the reality of urban decline and the simple fact that post-modernism can easily fade into neoliberalism and post-fordism.

Several studies have pointed to the emergence of the global city in which there has been a displacement of urban commu-nities and a reorganization of space. Saskia Sassen (1992) in *The Global City*, a study of London, New York and Tokyo, claims that these cities have become centres of global finance capitalism which is based on informational and communication tech-nologies. In these new global economies the city has become a transnational actor no longer exclusively connected with its national context. Other studies have looked at the transformation of the city by globalization which has arisen along with the new capitalism. With regard to community, what is highlighted are developments such as gentrification, and, more recently, the revanchist city with its gated communities.

Gentrification has had a significant influence on reshaping urban communities all over North America and western Europe since the late 1970s. Although it has a largely pejorative meaning, the term had initially been used to refer to the tendency in major cities for the professional middle classes to move into former working-class or ethnic communities, which became depopulated. As a positive development it meant that the city would not be entirely abandoned for the suburb, as had been the tendency in the preceding decades, and that urban neighbourhoods might be sustained by a prosperous and aesthetically conscious middle class, albeit one that was benefiting from relatively cheap real estate. In this sense, gentrification has been a reversal of suburbanization. In the view of many commentators, especially in the USA, gentrification leads to new urban communities that are affluent, cultural and ecological. Until it met with major opposition and eventually went into decline, gentrification was even compared to the expansion of the western frontier (Smith, 1996).[3] The gentrifiers were the new urban heroes rescuing the city from decline and for many town planners gentrification was even seen as a means of urban regeneration.

The reality of gentrification however is that it was closer to an invasion of the professional middle class and led to a considerable amount of population displacement, which followed rather than preceded gentrification. In other words, gentrification itself led to population displacement and was an expression of the emerging new capitalism in the wake of the disappearance of the traditional working class. For its critics, gentrification was a commodification of urban space and an ideology of postmodern consumption which announced that cities were uninhabitable and had to be revitalized around middle-class notions of taste. In this view the gentrifiers were the new class of postmoderns, a yuppified 'housing class'.[4] An example of this may be alternative neighbourhoods that evolved around community activism and the emergence of new social groups, such as localities identified with the gay community. The contribution of gentrification to community building will continue to be debated but its association with colonization and 'new class' wars is irreversible. According to Neil Smith, gentrification is part of postmodern late capitalism: 'Gentrification, and the redevelopment of which it is a part, is a systematic

occurrence of late-capitalist urban development. Much as capitalism strives towards the annihilation of space and time, it also
strives more and more to produce a differentiated space as a means
to its own survival' (Smith, 1996, p. 89).

Gentrification inevitably led to conflicts over the restructuring
of urban space, and in the view of several critics a yet newer
kind of class struggle has broken out with the declining significance of gentrification in the 1990s. Neil Smith speaks of the
subsequent rise in the post-gentrification era in the 1990s as
the 'revanchist city', where the middle classes have become more
concerned with security than with anything else. Revanchism –
a culture of class warfare using new instruments of control – is an
expression of the resentment of the gentrified middle class who
are now in a 'post-gentrification era'. There has been a reversal of
the earlier process of gentrification, for now the middle class are
'victims'. The truth is the gentrification has come and gone.
Gentrification was a product of the restructuring of the city since
the 1970s but today, since the 1990s, other forces have come into
play which have forced the affluent middle class on to the
defensive. This amounts to an acknowledgement of urban decline
in the emergence of new urban frontiers. As Neil Smith argues,
the new urban frontier is a closed one, in contrast to the open one
of gentrification. A new property market – 'Manhattanization' –
and declining state provision for local communities has put an
end to gentrification. Urban residential space is becoming highly
commodified and globalized, with buyers coming from all parts
of the world and paying huge sums of money for real estate which
is no longer affordable for the gentrifiers (Williams and Smith,
1986). Rising crime, violence, smog, unemployment and new
waves of immigration, often illegal, has forced out the white and
older ethnic communities leaving the middle class stranded in
what are rapidly becoming areas of urban decline.

> More than anything else the revanchist city expresses a race/
> class/gender terror felt by middle- and ruling-class whites who

are suddenly stuck in place by a ravaged property market, the threat of minority and immigrant groups, as well as women, as powerful urban actors. It portends a vicious reaction against minorities, the working class, homeless people, the unemployed, women, gays and lesbians, immigrants.

(Smith, 1996, p. 211)

Urban sociologists such as Mike Davis see such developments as amounting to the end of the city and with it the very possibility of community. In his books *City of Quartz: Excavating the Future in Los Angeles* (1990) and, especially, *Ecology of Fear: Los Angeles and the Imagination of Disaster* (1999) Davis describes in graphic detail the fragmentation of the city in an age of urban and ecological terror. His depiction of Los Angeles as the 'hard edge of the developers' millennium' is a striking contrast to the image of Chicago in the classical sociology of the Chicago School (Davis, 1990, p. 11). Especially since the racial riots in 1992 following the acquittal of four police officers for the now famous assault on Rodney King, Los Angeles has become the symbol of the anti-city. One of the current dominant motifs is the added factor of fear to the cityscape. 'The rhetoric of urban reform persists, but the substance is extinct. "Rebuilding L.A" simply means padding the bunker. As city life grows more feral, the various social milieux adopt security strategies and technologies according to their means' (Davis, 1999, p. 364). In a slightly futuristic portrayal of Los Angeles as the city of the future, we see a militaristic city emerging where the different income groups take responsibility for their own security. In this dystopian cityscape, Davis goes far beyond his evocation of Los Angeles in his earlier work, *City of Quartz. Ecology of Fear* depicts a city based on a fragmented world of spatially segregated groups, containment zones for the various sub-classes of permanently excluded low-skilled immigrant workers where crime and violence are very high, gated affluent suburbs, neighbourhood watches and community policing committees, booming edge cities, and an outer 'gulag rim' consisting of prisons. In this city-scape, community has retreated to the gated affluent suburbs where the middle class try to recover the lost Eden of the 1950s suburb.

Gated communities are highly protected enclaves for the white middle class who have embraced what Juan Perea (1996) has called a 'new nativism'. They are virtual 'fortresses' where the different segments of the white middle class have retreated. There is of course nothing entirely new in the spatial segregation of the classes. Urban planning since the mid-nineteenth century, as in Haussmann's redesign of Paris or the construction of sanitation areas in the industrial cities of England, aimed to separate the classes. Many merchant houses in Georgian England, with their stepped entrances and railings, were designed to withstand urban riots. However, what is new is the extent of the segregation bolstered by surveillance, exclusion zones and the abandonment by the state of the inner city, the modernist dream having been sundered. Even gentrification was based on the belief in commu-nity. The urban fortresses described by Davis are based on an 'ecology of fear' rather than on community trust and solidarity. These gated communities, where over three million Americans live, are literally closed, fortified enclaves with guards and gates and in which a kind of private community may be found. Outside these protected zones are other islands such as shopping malls which reinforce the spatial fragmentation of urban community. Gated communities exist in many American cities, for example, the 'white circle leagues' in Chicago, as well as in cities in the developing world.[5]

Outside the cities and their gated communities, a similar development in the USA is the creation of affluent communities, such as the suburb of Seaside in Florida. Leonie Sandercock refers to this as 'the New Urbanism' that aims to realize a utopia for the very rich that abandons the city altogether: 'It seeks to create instant community through design' (Sandercock, 1998, p. 194).

Perhaps something akin to a make-believe community identity exists in these artificial islands, but in the ghettos of 'containment zones' the basis of community identity does not exist.

EMPOWERING URBAN COMMUNITIES

Much of contemporary urban sociology paints a very negative picture of the city. In Mike Davis's work on the ecology of fear this takes on almost apocalyptic proportions. In contrast to this approach which takes postmodern Los Angeles as the image of the city for the twenty-first century, other approaches see the urban community in a more differentiated light. Not only is Los Angeles an exception in the USA, the American experience has not been entirely reflected in Europe. For instance, Loïc Wacquant has argued that there are still major differences between the deteriorated *banlieues* in France and the 'inner cities' in the USA. Ghettoization in France takes a different form and generalization on the basis of the American experience cannot be made (Wacquant, 1992, 1993, 1999).

There is much to suggest that the European city has many opportunities to assert its identity. European integration certainly offers many occasions for cities to recover their identity and provide opportunities for citizenship (Delanty, 2000c). To the extent to which cities can connect with other cities and not depend on national governments, the global society can offer local communities many possibilities. Castells thus sees European integration as offering many opportunities for local government. 'The more national states fade in their role, the more cities emerge as a driving force in the making of a new European society' (Castells, 1994, p. 23). The work of Manuel Castells is a good example of a sociological approach to the city that sees globalization offering new opportunities for the city. While he has always stressed the dangers of 'the dual city' that has come with post-fordism and the new information-driven economy, this does not exclude alternatives, for the city and even New York is a more open structure than the motif of the dual city, he suggests. Thus, while having some basis to it in changes in the occupational system and in the organization of residential space, the dual city is not the end of the city (Mollenkopf and Castells, 1991). In his many studies on the impact of globalization on the city, Castells believes the city can be reinvented (Castells, 1983, 1989, 1994; Borgja and Castells, 1997). This is because globalization is not necessarily destructive of local communities but can empower them. Aware of the corrosive and homogenizing consequences of globalization, Castells has been influential in giving an alternative to the pessimistic visions of the city discussed in the previous section. In earlier works, in opposition to classical Marxism, he argued that capitalism is more likely to be resisted by community-based activism than by work-based movements (Castells, 1977, 1978).

As discussed in Chapter 6, social movements can give rise to new expressions of community. Through participation in social movements, people discover they have common interests out of which collective identities can emerge. Drawing from decades of research into urban social movements, Castells argues that urban social movements, which are to be understood as processes of purposive social mobilization, have three main goals: 'urban demands on living conditions and collective consumption; the affirmation of local cultural identity; and the conquest of local political economy and citizen participation' (Castells, 1996, p. 60). These goals may of course be combined in different ways to produce a societal impact. An important insight is that 'regardless of the explicit achievement of the movement, its very existence produced meaning, not only for the movement's participants, but for the community at large' (Castells, 1996, p. 61). For Castells, the production of meaning is a central aspect both to social movements and to cities. Meaning is produced in conflicts between the interests of different groups but also in providing resistance to the one-sided logic of capitalism, statism and fundamentalism. The result is a paradoxical resurgence of local politics in a global era (see Chapter 8 on the local–global nexus). Urban movements and their discourses, actors and organizations are becoming more and more integrated into local governments as a result of citizens participation. This has tended to reduce the radical nature of these movements but on the other side has strengthened local governments. Another aspect is that while many of these movements have cultivated a 'not in my backyard' (or 'NIMBY') when it comes to issues around the disposal of toxic waste, prisons, nuclear plants and housing projects, this contains at least two dimensions. Such community responses may be defensive and reactionary or they may be progressive in wanting to preserve a form of life based on human ecology that is under threat from systemic forces. Another aspect to community renewal is that in many parts of the world, especially in the developing world, community can be a basis for alternative welfare regimes. Local communities, often with the aid of churches, have built their own welfare states in order to combat exploitation and poverty. Finally, Castells sees in local community, too, the dark side of urban warfare, with the large parts of many cities in America and the developing world in the control of gangs.

Thus in contrast to Mike Davis, Manuel Castells adopts an approach that comes close to the notion of the global village. It is, in general, a view that sees urban community as being enhanced by globalization. Janet Abu-Lughod's work on New York's Lower East Side represents a different perspective to both Castells and, especially, Davis (Abu-Lughod, 1994a). Arguing against a view that sees the urban community as a homogeneous voice of resistance and disagreeing with the opposite extreme that would see the city as depleted of agency and the capacity for resistance based on the power of community, she proposes a much more differentiated analysis. In this she comes close to Castells, but does not agree with the view that globalization itself offers a source of resistance. One of the leading urban sociologists, Janet Abu-Lughod's view of local community is one that stresses neither the old-fashioned urban village approach (e.g. of Robert Redfield) nor Castells' global village. In the oldest quarter of Manhattan, close to the financial district, one of the most enduring urban struggles has taken place in the resistance of a multicultural working class to gentrification. Abu-Lughod rejects the 'concept of the singular embattled defensive "community" where empowerment may be defined as a simple matter of "giving to the people what they want." Determining what "they" want (and what each player can get) is indeed the essential problematique of agency and local politics' (Abu-Lughod, 1994b, pp. 335–6). In contrast to Mike Davis' 'ecology of fear', Abu-Lughod's point of departure is an 'ecology of games'.[6] Recognizing that the 'local community of games' does not take place in a vacuum but is shaped by many forces of a structural nature, her contention is that these forces influence but do not shape the outcome of social struggles. In this approach that strongly emphasizes the power of community as agency, some generalizations can also be made on the basis of a case study. Processes of colonization, resistance, conflict and negotiation researched in this case study may be found in other diverse and changing inner cities, she argues. Despite this different emphasis in Abu-Lughod's work, she shares with Castells a strong emphasis on the politics of space and the role of local movements rooted in place rather than in an underlying cultural identity. The upshot of the new urban sociology looked at here – Neil Smith, Mike Davis, Manuel Castells, Janet Abu-Lughod – is a fresh thinking about social space.[7]

Edward Soja is a key theorist who has written extensively on alternative spatial structures for community. His notion of 'third space' aims to be an alternative to the two dominant conceptions of space that have prevailed, namely spatiality as concrete material forms to be mapped and controlled, and, on the other side, space as purely representational, as a cognitive construct

(Soja, 1996). Going beyond these notions of space – 'real' versus 'imagined' space – he argues for the creative openness of a 'third space'. Although this is formulated in very abstract terms, with references to Foucault's notion of 'heterotopologies' and 'other spaces', the work of Lefebvre, and theories of marginality, the idea approximates to a recovery of what Lefebvre called 'lived space'. His approach is to find examples of 'third space' even in the most unlikely of situations, for instance, in Los Angeles. We will not pursue this here, as our concern is with local community in urban contexts while much of the new urban social theory is driven by different issues.

Richard Sennett's work is a good starting point. One of the themes in his writing on cities over the past three decades has been the challenge of rehumanizing the city. Local community presents a problem in this task: 'Is it more effective to challenge the new capitalism from without, in the places where it operates, or seek to reform its operations from within?' (Sennett, 1998, p. 137). Fear of losing what they have become dependent upon leads citizens to refrain from challenging the corporations that have colonized local communities. On the other side, the new capitalism is sensitive to location, despite the flexibility of labour and capital. Place has power, Sennett argues, and the new capitalism can be constrained by it.

> One of the unintended consequences of modern capitalism is that it has strengthened the value of place, arousing a longing for community. All the emotional conditions . . . in the workplace animate that desire: the uncertainties of flexibility; the absence of deeply rooted trust and commitment; the superficiality of teamwork; most of all, the spectre of failing to make something of oneself in the world, to 'get a life' through one's work. All these conditions impel people to look for some other sense of attachment and depth.
>
> (Sennett, 1998, p. 138)

Thus the 'we' is a protective strategy and the desire for community is largely defensive, and for that reason can easily take authoritarian forms, as in the rejection of immigrants and other perceived 'outsiders'.[8] For all these reasons Sennett says community can be dangerous; yet it is necessary since social relations require mutual dependence. The task therefore is to design social institutions in a way that will foster trust and solidarity.

In this context there are several initiatives that can be commented on. Local community can be strengthened by strategies that enhance participation and self-sustainment such as ecologically sustainable policies, science shops, provision of goods and services, caring communities, community policing and community radio. The effective use of urban space and the minimization of consumption is important for ecological reasons and can also be a basis for creating ecologically sustainable communities. The challenge is thus to create forms of community within a framework of sustainability. The community application of expertise (science shops), recycling initiatives, re-greening zones, community land trusts can be the basis of alternative and strong local communities in which social capital is linked with ecological consciousness. Ecologically sustainable communities are also those that are self-organizing, supported by community-based planning (Sandercock, 1998).[9] As a result of the new capitalism, the number of shops and other retail outlets has dropped over the past twenty years, with the result that local communities have been greatly undermined in their infrastructure. Reversing this trend set by the big supermarkets will be crucial in building self-sufficient local communities and reducing dependency on car travel. Community radio has also been a significant means of enhancing community participation by offering opportunities for discursive participation that the national media cannot. Unlike the national media, community media is dialogic.

The turn to community is most evident in the area of community health. While the idea of the caring community has lost its association with an alternative to the formal, institutional one since informal networks can never be a substitute for state provision, in many respects – in particular for the mentally ill and the elderly – it is of continued relevance and an important part of local community development.[10] Community health initiatives, which involve local participation, have played an important role in empowering community, although such projects can also be a means of facilitating 'third-way' style policies which see the recipient as a consumer of services (Mayo, 2000, p. 158). Nevertheless, the turn to community development has been highly successful in many countries, and especially in the UK.[11] It has led to a more communicative kind of community which is capable of challenging capitalism and providing alternatives.

The capacity of local community to provide an alternative to the social fragmentation brought about by global capitalism cannot rest on social institutions alone. Important as these are in empowering local communities, the future of community will have to rest on the cultivation of what might be called a new language. Returning to an earlier theme in this book, only by generating communication communities can the demoralization of life and the social pathologies of the city be overcome. Institutions cannot offer new models of social integration when the foundations of community life are absent or have seriously disintegrated. The increase in demoralization, in depression, suicide, violence has led to a situation in which people no longer share a common language through which to communicate their experiences of deprivation, disrespect and the absence of 'recognition'. This has been argued by Axel Honneth, Pierre Bourdieu, Nancy Fraser and Richard Sennett for whom the task is to create a new 'habitus' or language in which collective experiences may be articulated.[12] Work in the flexible economy has made many people superfluous and with this goes a feeling of an absence of recognition.

Creating discourses for the expression of communicative competencies would appear to be one of the main challenges facing community today. As a communicative medium, community is still an important source of articulating less shared values or place than moral experiences. In order to build up self-esteem, self-respect and autonomous human beings, community needs to be more discursively mobilized. Local communities must be able to give voice to personal identities, rather than being seen as a cultural expression of collectivities or spatial categories to be organized into recipients of state services. This is more than a task for community alone; it is also a part of citizenship which may be conceived of as a learning process. It concerns the task of learning to give new definitions to work, social relations and the material environment. As a consciousness-raising discourse, in which flexibility might be challenged by reflexivity, community can become an important means of empowerment.

CONCLUSION

In this chapter the focus was on local community, as opposed to political community and cultural community. Local community is one of the major expressions of community and a central question in all discussions of local community is whether the urban form of the city accommodates it. We explored some of the debates on this question and found that while cities have become more *Gesellschaft*-based, they are none the less important containers of community. The pessimism and despair about the city in much of American sociology has led to an over-emphasis on revanchism and extreme forms of ghettoization. Loïc Wacquant (1999) is thus correct to criticize the way in which America has served as a 'social dystopia' for Europe when in fact the reality is much more differentiated in both America and especially in Europe. The work of Manual Castells and Janet Abu-Lughod was referred to in the context of community as empowerment.

In this regard what is of relevance is the idea of community as communication. Community is communicative in the sense of being formed in collective action based on place, and is not merely an expression of an underlying cultural identity. Local communities are important vehicles for the recovery and expression of moral recognition and the building of personal identities. There is an urgent need for such kinds of community today, since the flexible economy and the fragmentation of the social order have become more evident than ever before. The idea of community this points to is a constructivist one, whereby community is socially constructed by society as opposed to being identified simply with a locality.[13] In the example given of the study by Janet Abu-Lughod and her team of researchers on the battle for New York's Lower East Side, cultural differences were in fact the basis of the collective identity of the multi-cultural working class resisting the 'Manhattanization' of the locality. This suggests a view of community as a basis for the raising of a political consciousness.

4

POLITICAL COMMUNITY
Communitarianism and citizenship

Anthony Giddens has written: 'On each side of the political
spectrum today we see a fear of social disintegration and a
call for a revival of community' (Giddens, 1994, p. 124). What
Giddens has noted is that community has become a political
theme in both right and left political discourse today. In this
chapter we look at the debate on community in recent political
thinking. Unlike the sociological theory of community discussed
in the previous two chapters, the concept of community in
political philosophy has been largely of a normative nature, and
in some conceptions with considerable and growing influence
on policy-making in the English-speaking world. The main
sociological theories concerned the wider context of the transformation of modern societies, while in political philosophy the
question has largely been about the civic foundations of the polity.
For this reason much of the debate has been about citizenship,
which concerns membership of the polity. But the sociological

arguments about community discussed in Chapter 3 and the idea of community in political philosophy are not as entirely separate as they appear. What unites them is a view of community as being primarily about belonging. While much of the classical debate in sociology tended to stress tradition and locality, community in political philosophy has a broader concern. Yet arguably, both are about different expressions of community. In the case of Robert Bellah's major work *Habits of the Heart*, this connection between sociology and political philosophy is very evident (Bellah *et al.*, 1996). Here questions of the nature of the self, values and community are empirically investigated in a study that may be seen as a sociological version of communitarian political philosophy. In this work community is a mode of belonging and consists in desires and beliefs rather than in a territorial or institutional structure. Philip Selznick, in one of the major communitarian texts, describes community simply as a variable aspect of group experience (Selznick, 1992, p. 358). There are certainly advantages in this definition, especially in that it leaves open the possibility of community taking different forms. The communitarian position however differs from the conceptions of community discussed in the previous chapter in one major respect. Community is more than communitas or communion, but embraces a range of activities. What is particularly important, in Selznick's view, is participation, but also loyalty, solidarity and commitment. In the terms of, for instance, Victor Turner's theory of community, discussed in Chapter 2, communitarians are interested less in spontaneous, anti-structural community than in a normative theory of political community.

What has become known as communitarianism is a broad stance on citizenship that modifies considerably the previously dominant liberal position. The communitarian turn may be summed up in the phrase, 'from contract to community'.[1] Communitarians argue that citizenship is based on a social concept of the individual as a member of a community. Community in this sense means the civic community of the polity as opposed to a small-scale traditional community. However, in the most influential version of communitarianism, such as Charles Taylor's, this civic conception of community is ultimately a culturally codified type of community. In some interpretations it is often defined in terms of a minority group.

With communitarianism, community has become a highly contested term and even within communitarianism there are several strands. In many books and discussions on community the term is never defined, and consequently it is not easy to say exactly who is a 'communitarian'. In the following analysis I distinguish four main versions of communitarianism. The first is liberal communitarianism, as associated with the political philosophy of Michael Sandel and Michael Walzer, with a later strand in the more well-known communitarianism of Charles Taylor, and also includes new concerns with the cultural rights of national communities.[2] The second kind of communitarianism is what I call radical pluralism, which is characterized by an emphasis on group rights as opposed to the liberal patriotism of the former. Marion Iris Young and feminist theorists can be associated with this version. A third version is civic republicanism, or civic communitarianism, as represented by such figures as Robert Bellah, Philip Selznick, Robert Putnam and David Miller. In these works the emphasis is more on participation in civil society and social capital than on purely cultural conceptions of community. Finally, there is the governmental communitarianism of much of public policy which may also be associated with the writings of Etzioni. In this tradition, community is a governmentalized discourse.

LIBERAL COMMUNITARIANISM

The position that may be designated liberal communitarianism emerged as a modification of liberal political theory. The seminal works establishing communitarian thought have argued strongly against either the market or the state as the main focus for political community. More specifically communitarianism has opposed moral individualism in favour of a more social conception of the person. Communitarianism has inevitably defined itself in opposition to the two main liberal political theories: the social liberalism of John Rawls and the market liberalism of neoconservatism. Despite the centrality of the latter, rather strangely, the main opponent of communitarianism has been Rawls' version of liberalism. In *Liberalism and the Limits of Justice*, Michael Sandel (1982) argued that liberalism in the classical tradition – which he sees as culminating in the work of Rawls – neglects the social nature of the individual as a member of a community. While liberals see the individual as relatively autonomous, communitarians argue for the priority of the group. They reject moral individualism, which they see exemplified in Rawls' famous work *A Theory of Justice*, in favour of a deeper notion of community (Rawls, 1971). This position has been consolidated by such works as Michael Walzer's *Spheres of Justice*, Alasdair MacIntyre's *After Virtue*, Philip Selznick's *The Moral Commonwealth* and Charles Taylor's 'The Politics of Recognition' and *Sources of the Self*.[3]

Initially these positions were quite polarized to the extent that liberalism and communitarianism have often been seen as two quite distinct positions. However, it makes more sense to see communitarianism as a modification of liberalism than as distinct positions. For this reason communitarianism is best termed liberal communitarianism.[4] Both liberalism and communitarianism have been transformed by each other and in the case of the former by opposition to neoconservatism.[5] In the version of liberalism represented by Rawls, the concern from the beginning was more with social justice than with classical liberalism. In his later work *Political Liberalism* (Rawls, 1993) and *A Law of Peoples* (Rawls, 1999), Rawls recognized that some of the assumptions of his early position had to be modified, in particular the assumption of a cultural consensus on a common conception of the good. In these later works, there is a growing concern with the problem of community and the cultural foundations of the liberal polity. It also became more and more apparent as the debate progressed that there are not substantive differences between liberalism, in the version represented by Rawls, and communitarianism. Communitarians for their part have also made clear that they are not hostile to individualism as such. Where they differ ultimately is in certain questions on the ontological foundations of society, with communitarianism being primarily a demand for the recognition of a social ontology to correct the excessive concern with moral individualism in mainstream liberal political theory.

In any case, the early debate between liberals and communitarians around the foundations of the liberal polity was overshadowed in the 1990s by a debate about cultural rights. In this debate, in which Charles Taylor has been central, the issue is to what extent should the state bestow official recognition of certain groups in the society. Communitarianism as a 'politics of recognition',[6] to use the phrase that has come to characterize it, has in fact shifted on to new terms and the main protagonists are Taylor and Habermas, the latter occupying the place of Rawls in the debates of the 1980s.[7] In this turn, liberal communitarianism has made explicit its endorsement of certain kinds of nationalism. The idea of the nation or the national community has figured more centrally in Taylor's work and, in the form of liberal patriotism, has been at the centre of many studies of nationalism and populism in recent years.

Taylor is no ardent nationalist of course, and is cautious about polarizing the principles of equality, as advocated by mainstream liberalism, and difference, as advocated by communitarians. What he stands for is a liberal communitarianism that seeks to modify liberalism by compelling it to accommodate the reality of cultural difference and the need for the preservation of cultural community. Yet the differences between liberals and communitarians are quite strong. Because of the atomism underlying it, liberalism for Taylor has no sense of a common good in the narrow sense of a common way of life because society must be neutral about such values. Liberalism however does recognize a common good in the broader sense of a commitment to procedures, rules and generally a formal means of 'agreeing to differ'. But for Taylor there is also a common good in the more specific substantive sense of 'patriotism', an identification with a political community which itself embodies a deeper cultural way of life. In essence, Taylor differs from liberals and those of a broadly liberal disposition such as Habermas, who argue for a purely formal or procedural kind of political community, in claiming that community must also be based on a substantive moment and consequently the state cannot be neutral.

For Taylor, in the case of culturally divided societies – such as Canada – it is vital for the state to grant official recognition to the different groups. The politics of recognition is thus a politics of group differentiation. What is at issue is a particular conception of the collective self and it is one that is frequently defined in terms of minority or majority status within the polity. For Taylor, who stresses language as the embodiment of community, the self is always culturally specific. For this reason his version of communitarianism may be seen as a defence of cultural particularism against the moral universalism of liberalism, be it in the work of Rawls or in the communicative universalism of Habermas.[8]

The politics of recognition can take the form of an emphasis on equality – the equal dignity of all citizens with respect to their rights and moral worth – or an emphasis on difference, where what is significant is the need of the majority culture to make concessions to particular groups, generally minorities: 'Where the politics of universal dignity fought for forms of nondiscrimination that were quite "blind" to the ways in which citizens differ, the politics of difference often redefines nondiscrimination as requiring that we make these distinctions the basis of differential treatment' (Taylor, 1994, p. 39). His argument is that in order for a cultural community to retain its integrity and flourish in the face of a majority there must be some public recognition by the state of cultural community. But there is little doubt that Taylor is arguing only for certain large-scale groups, such as the French-speaking Canadians in Quebec, to retain their autonomy. It would appear that real recognition for liberal communitarianism is recognition of a self-declared majority capable of defining the common good. So long as this culture respects diversity, it has a reasonable claim to official recognition.

As already noted for communitarians, the basic ideas of liberalism are not in question. While their preference is clearly for a positive recognition of cultural community, this is anchored in a basic commitment to the liberal principle of equality. Liberal communitarianism is not a radical theory of group difference but a modification of liberalism's moral individualism and above all of the idea of the culturally neutral constitution. While liberals get around the problem of protecting minority groups by a commitment to group rights (Kymlicka, 1995), communitarians on the whole are more concerned with protecting the majority culture which is not an issue for liberals, since this is largely taken for granted; or, as in a recent formulation by Rawls, it is a matter of looking for an 'overlapping consensus'.[9] Thus it appears that what began as a concern with the search for a social ontology has culminated in a defence of cultural community. In this respect, the liberal ethos may be stretched too far, for as Zygmunt Bauman has argued, the liberal idea of 'difference' stands for individual freedom, while the communitarian 'difference' stands for the group's power to limit individual freedom (Bauman, 1993). It would be nonsense to claim that communitarianism stands for cultural authoritarianism, but it is evident that it may lead to illiberal conclusions, for the concept of community in communitarian discourse is the community of the dominant culture which is officially recognized by the state. The assumption is that political community must rest on a prior cultural community and that minorities and incoming groups to the polity must adapt to this cultural community. This is precisely what is objected to by radical pluralists.

RADICAL PLURALISM

Liberal communitarianism has been limited by an implicit concern with justifying a certain kind of patriotism. In this it has not been a major departure from classical liberalism, since many liberal philosophers and politicians have supported nationalism. J.S. Mill – in his *Considerations on Representative Government* in 1861 – was in favour of nationalism, and William Gladstone, the British liberal politician, supported nationalist movements in the second half of the nineteenth century, ranging from Irish home rule nationalism to the cause of Bulgarian nationalism. Today communitarianism has exemplified the cause of liberal nationalism, and in its most influential forms it has amounted to demands for cultural rights as a basis of citizenship. It is possible to identify an alternative and radical strand within communitarianism which may be called radical pluralism. This takes as its point of departure the idea of difference, which has made its entry with liberal communitarianism. But the relatively conservative concerns characteristic of much of liberal communi-tarianism do not figure in what in fact is a radical pluralist theory of community in which community is seen as overlapping and contested.

Rejecting both liberalism and patriotism, radical pluralists place cultural or group-based rights on a different footing altogether.[10] This development in what in only a very general sense belongs to the communitarian movement is very much the result of feminism, and many of its most well-known advocators are feminist theorists (Benhabib, 1992, 1996; Frazer and Lacey, 1993; Lister, 1997, 1998; Young, 1989, 1990, 2000). These theorists have argued for a group differentiated understanding of community, which is never holistic. Thus in the work of Marion Iris Young – where the communitarian position is more strongly evident than in other radical pluralists – community is reconceived around group differences within the broader society. In the recent work of Michael Walzer there is a nuanced recognition of 'thin' as opposed to 'thick' forms of community (Walzer, 1994).

The essential issue in these debates concerns the problem of empowering marginal groups. Whereas for liberal communitarians, such as Will Kymlicka, it is mostly a matter of self-government rights for large-scale minorities, for radical pluralists such as Marion Young the problem is to shape a genuine multicultural society where all groups may be accommodated, regardless of their size and importance. Liberal communitarians make clear that they are concerned only with the level of state recognition. Moreover, such expressions of cultural rights confine the politics of citizenship to the public domain. Radical pluralists go further in demanding the extension of citizenship into the private realm. According to Young, citizenship is more than participation and rights in the public domain but must also entail rights in the private realm, in issues such as gender, age and disability. Marion Young argues that

> we need a group differentiated citizenship and a heterogeneous public. In a heterogeneous public, differences are publicly recognised and acknowledged as irreducible, by which I mean that persons from one perspective or history can never completely understand and adopt the point of view of those with other group-based perspectives and histories.

> (Young, 1989, p. 258)

With radical pluralism, the ideal of equality that was basically accepted by liberal communitarianism has been diminished considerably by a more explicit emphasis on difference. In later chapters of this book this theme of community and difference will be taken up (especially in Chapter 6). However, the emphasis on difference in this more radical strand within communitarianism is best characterized as radical pluralism. While Iris Young adheres to certain aspects of communitarianism, this is not true of Nancy Fraser and Seyla Benhabib and others for whom the critical issue is democracy. Essential to democracy is the negotiation of difference and the avoidance of the communitarian descent into relativism and the moral universalism of liberalism. Radical pluralism does not dispense with community, here understood as ties of belonging and identity. Community is a communicative category rather than a closed cultural sphere which cannot be neglected by democracy.

CIVIC REPUBLICANISM

Communitarianism is not only about the politics of identity, but also concerns another dimension of citizenship, namely participation. While liberal and radical communitarianism, despite all their differences, were concerned mostly with cultural rights in the sense of special rights for groups, the civic tradition within communitarianism has made social capital and participation in public life central to community.

Civic republicanism – which may also be termed civic communitarianism – has often been traced back to the political thought of Jean-Jacques Rousseau in *The Social Contract* in 1743 where he argued for a radical conception of citizenship as popular participation in the polity. Civic republicanism may also be found in the work of theorists as diverse as Hannah Arendt (1958), Benjamin Barber (1984), Michael Oldfield (1990), John Pocock (1995), Robert Putnam (1993, 1999), Philip Selznick (1992),

John O'Neill (1994) and Robert Bellah *et al.* (1986). The civic republican tradition, like liberal communitarianism, may be seen as a radical form of liberal individualism, but differing from it in several respects. For civic republicans, individualism reaches its highest expression in public life, as opposed to the liberal emphasis on the private pursuit of interest or personal autonomy. In this sense it is closer to liberal communitarianism since what is stressed is community life. Rather than self-interest, what is at stake is public interest and collective goals. While liberalism was based on negative freedom – the right to be *from* something rather than the right *to* do something – the civic republican ideal of politics is one of positive freedom, as, for instance, in the ideal of a self-governing political community. For this reason it may be said that civic republicanism is based on an active concept of citizenship, in contrast to the passive model typical of liberalism. This active conception of politics as public engagement is the true meaning of republicanism, as intended by the radical stream within the Enlightenment, though it was only in America that it became a real force, as de Tocqueville recognized. In the radical variant, represented by Rousseau, this entailed a confrontation with liberal democracy, or constitutional democracy, in that the ideal of a self-governing political community was incompatible with representative government. It may be noted in this context that historically liberal democracy had been tied to constitutional monarchy. But for theorists such as Hannah Arendt, civic republicanism was perfectly compatible with representative government (Arendt, 1958). The challenge for civic republicanism rather lay in bringing politics out of the state and into the public domain.

One of the legacies of this tradition has been an ambivalent relationship with democracy. Like liberalism, classical republicanism preceded the democratic revolution and accommodated democracy to varying degrees. Several proponents trace it back to classical Greek thought and practice. As is evidenced in the writings of Hannah Arendt, republicanism exhibits a deep distrust of the modern idea of democracy which is associated with the intrusion of the social question into what is allegedly a purely political domain. However, the original inspiration of republicanism is a radical notion of citizenship as participation in civil society. The radical dimension of contemporary civic republicanism must not be exaggerated, for in many versions it is quite a conservative doctrine about participation in a culturally neutral civil society. In this sense civil society consists merely of associations and voluntary deeds.

Thus much of civic republicanism is a 'neo-Tocquevillean' discourse of the loss of community. For Robert Putnam, one of the most famous exponents of a civic kind of communitarianism, contemporary American society is characterized by a decline in community values, as measured by the decline in what he called 'social capital'. For many civic republicans community means the creation and mobilization of 'social capital'. Robert Putnam relates civic engagement with 'social capital', which takes over the role of cultural identity in Charles Taylor's communitarianism. The point about community is not its ability to overcome conflicts but to promote values of trust, commitment and solidarity, values which allow democracy to flourish. Social responsibility primarily falls firmly on the shoulders of civil society rather than on the state which, Putnam argues, can function only if civil society already speaks with one voice. In his study of modern Italy he thus found that what matters is not institutions but cultural traditions, in particular those that reinforce civil society (Putnam, 1993). It is civil society that makes for a better state and public institutions, not the reverse, he argues.

Putnam's conception of community is one that is nostalgic about the past, in particular the kind of American society that was based on Americans born between 1910 and 1940. He argues that with the passing of this generation the contemporary society is bereft of the spirit of community life that is essential for the cohesion of society. In his much discussed book *Bowling Alone*, he tells the story of 'the collapse of community' in contemporary America. Although his theme is also about the 'recovery' of community, the overall impression is one of the decline of social capital as a result of apathy, self-interest and disengagement from public life (Putnam, 1999). Americans now prefer to bowl alone rather than together in the local clubs and leagues. Whether it is bowling – the traditional American community sport – or other communal activities, such as local clubs, attending public meetings or parents' associations, or charity work, there is a decline of voluntarism and with this comes a decline in trust, without which modern societies cannot function, for trust is an essential feature of democracy. Individualism and above all the mass media, especially television, and changes in the nature of work, have destroyed community as measued by participation in associations; instead they have found meaning in personal pursuits, careers and consumption to the detriment of the collective values that sustain civic society.

This 'civic republican' argument may also be termed 'neo-Tocquevillean' in its claim that democracy is based on social capital.[11] Putnam's position ultimately is quite conservative in his assumption that a strong civil society will lead to a stronger state in which democracy will flourish. It is a position that ignores conflicts, instead seeing social capital as an affirmative resource that may be translated into government policy.[12] A similar position is to be found in the writings of the American cultural critic Christopher Lasch, who, in his final work, saw the decline of democratic values of citizenship as a consequence of the betrayal of democracy not by the masses but by the elites who have isolated themselves from community (Lasch, 1995).[13] Lasch's solution was a call to return to the virtues of community, religion and family. Much of civic republican thought tends to look backwards to the time when liberal Protestant values held American society together. One of the ideas behind this way of thinking is that democracy is based on fairly culturally homogeneous communities. Consequently the implication of communitarian theories is that the contemporary multicultural society is unable to sustain democratic citizenship. The result is that communitarianism, with its themes of the demise of community, social dysfunctionality, culture wars and weariness with modernity has become the inspiration for a great deal of recent American cultural criticism.

The belief in democratic community is central to *Habits of the Heart*, a widely read book written by the sociologist Robert Bellah and others and first published in 1986 (Bellah *et al.*, 1996). In this work the tone is less nostalgic, and community is seen as part of the lives of many people who draw upon it in everyday practices and through memories. There can be 'communities of memory' in ethnic, racial and religious groups as well as on the level of the nation and also within families. Such communities of memory are also 'communities of commitment', the authors argue. Community is kept alive not only in shared memories but also in practices of solidarity (Bellah *et al.*, 1996, pp. 153–4). Individualism and expressiveness undermine but do not erode community. Unlike Putnam's emphasis on the decline of social capital, the message is that community is alive and well, sustaining individualism despite all appearances to the contrary. There is also another sense in which their work differs from Putnam's. The authors of *Habits of the Heart* are critical of the prospect that small-scale communities based on voluntary groups can solve the major problems of society. They also note that voluntarism is generally to be found in the better-off strata and thus does not really help the deprived, especially in American society where there is greater class and ethnic segregation. However, in the second edition in 1996, there is a stronger sense of the decline of social capital and, as a consequence, a decline in political engagement. But they stress that the causes of this are less individualism than neo-capitalist economic developments.

This critical perspective is much stronger in the work of Richard Sennett. Civic republican themes can be found in his writings, such as *The Fall of Public Man*, but he is in general more critical of communitarianism (Sennett, 1978). In *The Corrosion of Character* he heavily criticizes communitarianism which is based, he argues, on a superficial sense of unity: 'Communitarianism in my view has a very dubious claim of ownership of trust or commitment; it falsely emphasizes unity as the source of strength in a community and mistakenly fears that when conflicts arise in a community, social bonds are threatened' (Sennett, 1998, p. 143). For Sennett, communitarianism stresses too much community as a moral solution to problems that are caused by capitalism and changes in the nature of work. A similar liberal-left-wing conception of community may be found in the work of the British political theorists David Miller and Paul Hirst. In *Markets, the State and Community* Miller defends the idea of community as a basis for a just society. Community is an indispensable foundation for democracy (Miller, 1989). Paul Hirst's work on associative democracy establishes a link between democracy and associational forms of organization while avoiding the excessive moral dimension that characterizes communitarianism (Hirst, 1994).

In sum, civic republican communitarianism emphasizes social capital as the defining tenet of community and which in turn is the basis of a functioning democracy. In general, the conception of social capital in this particular strand in communitarianism stresses its moral character and views the contemporary situation in terms of a decline in social capital. In contrast, other, more critically inclined approaches, such as Sennett's, see social capital as an important aspect of community but do not view it as a purely civic, moral set of values.

GOVERNMENTAL COMMUNITARIANISM

While liberal communitarianism (discussed earlier in this chapter) was largely a modification of liberalism in its advocacy of a politics of recognition for particular, and in fact culturally defined groups, communitarianism in recent times has become a more 'governmentalized' discourse. Community has become more central to 'third-way' style politics, which in turning away from social democracy finds in community a means of softening the move towards neo-capitalist restructuring. According to Nikolas Rose, adapting a Foucauldian analysis, 'in the institution of community, a sector is brought into existence whose vectors and forces can be mobilized, enrolled, deployed in novel programmes and techniques which encourage and harness active practices of self-management and identity construction, of personal ethics and collective allegiances. I term this government through community' (Rose, 1999, p. 176). This growing discourse of community in policy-making may be described, following Rose's suggestion, as a governmental communitarianism since its aim is to construct a political subjectivity through policy-making.

In the 1990s communitarianism became popular in Britain and North America, being frequently interchangeable with a civic patriotism.[14] It was central to the political rhetoric of the British Labour Party in the election campaign in 1997 when the terms 'nation' and 'society' became interchangeable but in a way that was a contrast to the authoritarian communitarianism of patriotic Toryism. The appeal to trust and solidarity as British civic values allowed the Labour Party to take over the Conservative Party's previous monopoly of the discourse of the nation. Communitarianism – as in Tony Blair's notion of a 'stakeholder's society' – served as a legitimation of a 'third-way' style of government. There had always been a strand of communitarianism in the British Labour Party and with the dilution of socialism the new 'third-way' discourse has made frequent use of overt communitarian themes. Perhaps because community is a vague term it can be adapted easily to a project that is devoid of ideological purpose and can fit into either right- or left-wing moulds.

According to Nikolas Rose, community has become a quasi-governmental discourse that facilitates new technologies of power and of social management. The new technologies of community are a diffuse set of practices regulated by community experts which cut across government and civil society, linking citizens to the state. Community becomes 'governmental' when it becomes 'technical', that is as a sector for government. In the political programmes of the Blair and, earlier, in the Clinton governments, corresponding to their 'third-way' politics, there is also a 'third space' in which the discourse of community is infused with notions of voluntarism, charitable works and self-organized care (Rose, 1999, p. 171). The attraction of community may be explained by its moral overtones, for the subject of community is one with civic obligations and moral commitments to society. This produces the political effect of disburdening the state of responsibility and diluting social citizenship. The governmentalization of community facilitates the creation of a whole array of discourses about community; for instance, community regeneration, community experts, and local community initiatives such as community policing, community safety and community development (Rose, 1999, p. 189). It is important not to see this as merely the exercise of social control, for it can also lead to community empowerment. The language of community and of morality is increasingly entering political discourse (i.e. ethical investment, ethical foreign policy). But as Rose points out this can be a superficial moralizing of politics or it can offer new possibilities for empowerment for an ethico-politics. Not too surprisingly, then, we find the discourse of community in the manifestos of the Clinton and Blair governments emphasizing voluntarism, charitable works and self-organized care (Rose, 1999, p. 171).

One of the most well-known writers on community is Amitai Etzioni (1995, 2001). Although not an explicitly governmental communitarianism but a variant of civic republicanism, his promotion of community approximates the official discourses of community in policy-making, as is suggested too by his quarterly, *The Responsive Community*, which is a major manifesto for American popular communitarianism. His advocation of community may be seen as an American reaction to the dominance of rational choice and neoliberalism in the 1980s. Community for Etzioni is essentially the moral foundation and the expression of a citizenship of responsibility and of participation, as opposed to one of rights. Community entails voice, a 'moral voice', and social responsibility rests on personal responsibility. A concern with responsibility articulates a core idea of Etzioni's communitarianism. Etzioni's conception of responsive community is rooted in 'social virtues' and 'basic settled values' (Etzioni, 1995, pp. 1–5). The family and the school are the typical institutions which can cultivate the kind of citizenship required by responsive community.

Etzioni is very vague on what constitutes a community, but it is clear that it does not include the political community of the state. His call for a recovery of community is an appeal to the little community of the neighbourhood, the locality, the family, associations. It is a view of community that is decidedly privatistic and which more or less absolves the state of responsibility for society. The connection with governmental community consists in concerns with issues relating to schooling, family and policing. This is a vision of community that is ultimately incompatible with diversity and social differentiation. Although he claims it is a post-traditional kind of community, and not a nostalgic return to the past, his idea of community is expressed very much in terms of personal proximity, locality, small groups and personal responsibility for society. The assumption made throughout his work is that consensus either exists or can be unproblematically created.

Governmental communitarianism is often a superficial politics of legitimacy. The appeal to community can be easily compatible with many different political positions, ranging from the right to the left. It is almost invariably another word for citizenship, but an aspect of citizenship that stresses less the entitled citizen than the dutiful citizen.

In sum, what I have termed *governmental communitarianism* reflects the assimilation of the discourse of community into official policy-making. It is also expressed in conservative conceptions of community, such as Etzioni's, where community articulates disciplinary strategies, such as community policing, neighbourhood watches, and a political subjectivity that does not seek large-scale solutions to social problems but rather looks to voluntarism.

CONCLUSION

The main themes in communitarianism are:

- the shift from social equality to cultural difference;
- social capital as the basis of democracy and citizenship;
- the definition of community as one of shared values, solidarity and attachments;
- a social ontology of group ties as opposed to moral individualism;
- a group differentiated conception of citizenship;
- an emphasis on cultural rights as opposed to social rights.

Two conclusions may be reached. First, communitarianism in general reflects a post-traditional conception of community. Second, although it has a post-traditional dimension its capacity for pluralization is limited. Mainstream communitarian thought highlights the civic and normative dimension of community, as opposed to the symbolic and liminal dimension discussed in Chapter 3. Resonances can certainly be found with Durkheim's civic communitarianism. However, in mainstream communitarianism the overwhelming impression is one of an affirmative stance on many issues. It is an anti-political kind of politics that appeals to moral sentiments and civic virtues. With the exception of radical pluralism, which is marginal and highly critical of mainstream communitarianism, the main varieties offer a conservative vision of society, stressing small groups, voluntarism and patriotism. Although communitarianism sees itself as offering contemporary society a post-traditional conception of community to combat the ills of modernity, there is a discourse of the loss of community running through many of the major works.[15]

Another notable shortcoming of communitarianism is that it holds to a view of community as based on self-contained, fairly homogeneous groups which are capable of agency. In fact, as will be demonstrated in Chapter 5, this view of group formation is fundamentally incompatible with the social reality of multiculturalism. There is no serious thought given to conflicts within community as opposed to the conflict between community and society, which is the major focus of communitarianism. Where this is not the issue, the problem becomes one of conflicts between communities, which tend to be seen as relatively homogeneous when in fact the reality of community is overlapping memberships, multiplicity of identities and allegiances. The general picture of community in communitarian thought is that culture is divisive and that contemporary societies are being torn apart by cultural conflicts. Chapter 5 looks at exactly this myth of cultural conflict as endemic to multiculturalism.

5

COMMUNITY AND DIFFERENCE
Varieties of multiculturalism

No discussion on community can avoid the question of multiculturalism. The analysis of communitarianism in the previous chapter indicated that much of communitarian thought is incompatible with multiculturalism. Those dimensions of communitarianism that do respond to the challenge of difference have stopped short of pluralization. In general communitarianism accepted difference only within certain limits. Multiculturalism, like community, is an essentially contested term taking many different forms. Communitarianism itself is a legitimation of one particular kind of multiculturalism but has problems in responding to other kinds of multiculturalism, and for this reason its appropriateness to the current situation must be questioned. Communitarianism however shares with the idea of multiculturalism the assumption which may no longer be tenable that there is a multiplicity of incommensurable cultural communities. For this reason, multiculturalism, at least in its dominant forms, may no longer be an appropriate model of understanding cultural community today.

The problem is that western multiculturalism has generally been based on the separation of the cultural from the social. Culture has been seen as a sphere of division and must be managed. In effect, multiculturalism was a means of managing cultural diversity arising from large-scale immigration into western societies that came in the wake of decolonization and waves of immigrant workers. European multiculturalism, as it emerged in the 1960s and 1970s, was essentially an extension of liberal tolerance rather than aiming at participation of immigrants in citizenship. It was based on the assumption that there was a dominant cultural identity, in the society to which the incoming ethnic groups had to adjust but to whom certain concessions could be made. Multiculturalism was never intended to be a model for bringing about wider change in society. In this sense, multiculturalism was not based on a communicative model of community but a civic one, in that its aim was merely the management of cultural diversity within the established structures. Like secularism in an earlier period of modernity, which protected religion by giving it a sheltered space outside the public domain, multiculturalism was a means of protecting the established society from the new cultural communities. But today it is a different matter, for after several decades and generational shifts, diversity has penetrated the cultural identity of the whole society. Integration today is becoming based increasingly on the individual, rather than on the community or group. Such a development, in fact, allows for more social integration than is often thought.[1]

Nevertheless multiculturalism continues to be a contested concept. The older models of multiculturalism assumed that common ground had to be limited to the public sphere given the alleged diversity of cultures, whereas more recent models have introduced the idea of group differentiated rights for large-scale organized groups. As a result of social change in recent years, such as growing transnationalism, pluralization and individuation, the presuppositions of multiculturalism have been undermined. Whether we can still speak of multiculturalism in referring to new forms of cultural community is an open question and will be addressed in this chapter. The central idea is that communities cannot be so easily defined in cultural terms, thus raising questions about the viability of multiculturalism. However, rather than reject the concept it is argued that a democratic, flexible kind of multiculturalism may be possible if the emphasis shifts to social issues.

In the following discussion the ten main models of multiculturalism are outlined and discussed. In this analysis multiculturalism is taken to be any major strategy aimed at managing cultural community, in particular insofar as this is defined in largely cultural terms. In essence, this means an understanding of community as defined as fairly cohesive ethnic groups. The main models of multiculturalism are: (1) monoculturalism, (2) republican multiculturalism, (3) pillarization, (4) liberal multiculturalism, (5) communitarian multiculturalism, (6) liberal communitarian multiculturalism, (7) interculturalism, (8) radical multiculturalism, (9) critical multiculturalism and (10) transnational multiculturalism. These models of multiculturalism are looked at in what follows under the headings of traditional multiculturalism, modern multiculturalism and post-multiculturalism.

TRADITIONAL MULTICULTURALISM

Under this heading we can include the older forms of multiculturalism, namely the first four models referred to above: monoculturalism, republican multiculturalism, pillarization and liberal multiculturalism.

Monoculturalism

Strictly speaking, monoculturalism is the opposite of multiculturalism since it privileges the cultural identity of the majority, making political identity coeval with a dominant ethnic cultural identity. It is in effect the denial of cultural diversity. Japanese citizenship is still based very much on this equation of ethnicity with nationality as a qualification for citizenship. A more pertinent European example might be illustrated by Germany where only one cultural identity has official recognition, for the national identity is coeval with an ethnic identity based on German descent. Thus in Germany, citizenship rests generally on German ethnicity rather than on birth, as in France. In the case of monocultural societies, cultural diversity can exist only at the margins of society. In such societies the aim of multiculturalism can only be integration rather than assimilation.

However, it is important to say that few countries that are officially monocultural do not have ways of promoting other kinds of multiculturalism, though this is unlikely to extend beyond partial citizenship. In Japan interculturalism (see below) has official existence and in Germany, despite the *jus sanguinis*,[2] communitarian multiculturalism is well established at regional levels.

Republican multiculturalism

The paradigmatic model of this is the French republican reduction of multiculturalism to the private sphere. In this model, as in the American tradition (discussed below), there can be no public recognition of cultural differences in the public domain of civil society which is supposed to be a domain of equality. The culture-blind model of multiculturalism assumes the absolute separation of cultural and political identity. Whereas the American model of assimilation sees the eventual aim of multicultural policy to be the creation of a common way of life, this classic republican policy (which may be called the 'salad-bowl' model as opposed to the American 'melting-pot' model) accepts the reality of diversity at the prepolitical level, seeking only a shared political identity. In France this comes from the republican ideology that there is only one political identity – the republican values of the constitution and guaranteed by the absolute neutrality of the state with respect to culture and all forms of ethnicity, be they those of the dominant groups in society or those of recent immigrants. Thus the kind of assimilation that it demands is a coercive one, for minority groups must deny their cultural traditions and effectively become French (Kastoryano, 2002; Wieviorka, 1998). In France where the republican ethos is most apparent, the multicultural society (as we know from the 'headscarves affair') quite literally ends at the school gates – for once the shared public domain of the state and its institutions is approached there can be no tolerance of diversity.

However, it must be added that this model, like the previous one, is rarely as inflexible as it is often claimed to be. In reality, as is witnessed by the ruling of the French Constitutional Court on the controversial headscarves case, the state will recognize the claims of a cultural group, although generally in a highly qualified way. But there is no denying the reality that the classic republican model has been diluted in practice by the interest of the state to move closer to a pluralist model of integration (Schain, 2000).

In general, the view is that multiculturalism resides primarily in the private sphere. That is, the prepolitical sphere of ethnic privatism or, as more recent developments might indicate, in the sphere of consumption in which the middle classes of the dominant groups participate in the multicultural society. In this sense, most western European countries are multicultural. But this is a prepolitical culturalism that was seen originally to reside in tolerance of ethnic groups. In time, with the incorporation of ethnic groups into society, multiculturalism came to be an expression of a society that had come to terms with multiple cultural identities and the key marker of multiculturalism resided in new patterns of consumption. Indeed, many societies – ones as different as Ireland and Japan, for instance – became multicultural through consumption rather than through ethnicity (in this case the kind of multiculturalism that is implied is closer to interculturalism, discussed later in this chapter).

Pillarization

As with the previous two models this is also a historical model but one that has ceased to exist today. In The Netherlands it was the official means of accommodating the two religious traditions within the polity. In The Netherlands the principle of the equality of religions has been accepted since the early nineteenth century. However, state support for Catholic schools was not granted until 1917, when the system known as pillarization was adopted formally as a means of organizing education into the Catholic and Protestant denominations, and for much of the twentieth century it was the official means of dealing with cultural pluralism. Originally this referred to the two main denominations, but from 1983, with the recognition that The Netherlands was a multicultural society, this principle was extended to the other religious traditions, such as the Jewish and Hindu groups. However, the model was limited because it was deemed to apply only to religious groups, not ethnic groups as such (Nederveen Pieterse, 1997, pp. 177–200). Moreover, as the term suggests, it was intended to be a means of negotiating the main 'pillars' of society – i.e. the main churches – and was thus ineffective in dealing with groups with lesser influence. Today, as a result of growing numbers of ethnic groups who are not defined primarily by religion, it is no longer regarded as an appropriate model for multiculturalism in what is also a predominantly secular society.

It may be noted in passing that the Ottoman 'millet system' by which certain non-Muslim minorities were officially recognized by the state and allowed to govern themselves was an earlier form of officially endorsed multiculturalism (Eisenberg, 1999, pp. 390–1). In the USSR there was also a similar policy of instituting ethnic citizenship within the federal republics. To an extent, Switzerland may be cited as a contemporary example of this kind of multiculturalism. However, in this case the groups in question are not minorities but subnational groups.

Liberal multiculturalism

This is the constitutional American paradigm, which has also been called the 'melting-pot' model. The basis of this is the view that all immigrants will become assimilated into the one society. Strictly speaking, this model is not a model of 'multiculturalism' since the aim is to have a common way of life – 'the American way of life' – and not the preservation of differences. It was based on the assumption of assimilable groups. Although often seen as the paradigmatic expression of multiculturalism, this model of multiculturalism is, in fact, very specific to the USA and rests on a curious teleology: American multiculturalism is based on the fact of diversity on the level of cultural identity and an absolute commitment to the neutrality of the shared public culture of the political domain. Liberalism in political identity and multiculturalism in ethnic identities was seen to provide the structures for the formation of a uniquely American way of life, for in time, it was believed, the mix of cultures would create a common way of life.

The neutrality of the political sphere of the state and the fact that, culturally, the USA was a society of immigrants made such a utopia possible (at least if we ignore the fact that the descendants of white Anglo-Saxon colonizers occupied the key positions in the society). While the circumstances peculiar to the USA – the large influx of immigrants, the absence of a native ruling elite – made this a reasonable expectation, the dream rested ultimately on the ability of the social structure to deliver the promise of a new society, and in this it was judged a failure by many (while being defended by many others) (Glazer and Moynihan, 1963; Hall and Lindholm, 1999; Schlesinger, 1992). In any case the widespread belief was that the mixing of cultures along with the core ideology of American society – meritocratic individualism – would lead to common ground.

The assumption of assimilation in the American tradition differs from the French policy in that it is less coercive and less based on the official identity of the constitutional state. It may be observed that while the American model had its roots in a modern society of immigrants, this republican model arose in a premodern Enlightenment society when religion, as the principal marker of cultural identity, was relegated to the private sphere. It is still in the mould of Enlightenment anti-clericalism that multiculturalism is cast as far as the constitutional national state is concerned.

However, exactly where the divide between multiculturalism as a process of assimilation and cultural diversity lies is not easy to specify. Ultimately, liberal constitutional democracy and multiculturalism are not compatible, since the former is based on equality and the latter on diversity. In any case, American multiculturalism today has little in common with the constitutional tradition, which has become, in the words of Daniel Lazare, 'frozen': the model of the 'melting-pot' has been superseded by radical multiculturalism and various kinds of communitarianism which do have universality as their overriding objective (Lazare, 1996). This is because the question today is no longer immigrants but race, and the need to make social institutions more representative of their environment. Moreover, many indigenous groups have won the right of self-government despite the culture-blindness of the American constitution, a fact that exemplifies the contemporary relevance of the constitutional tradition, according to James Tully (1995).

MODERN MULTICULTURALISM

The models of multiculturalism discussed in the previous section are all based on the refusal to recognize cultural difference. In this sense they are not strictly speaking models of multiculturalism since they regard cultural difference as something that needs to be eliminated. The following may be said to be the main models of multiculturalism: communitarian multiculturalism, liberal communitarian multiculturalism and interculturalism. What they all share is a recognition of the reality of cultural diversity and the need for pluralist policies.

Communitarian multiculturalism

Communitarianism is best represented by Canada, whose constitutional tradition is not based on classical liberal democracy. The accommodation of cultural diversity and democracy is not antithetical since they are in the republican constitutional traditions, as in France and the USA. This is a relatively recent conception of multiculturalism, although there have been historical cases of group differentiated citizenship, as, for example, rights the Amish community has won in the USA. In Canada, unlike the USA, immigration has played a more central role in the formation of society in the latter half of the twentieth century.

The Canadian federal state grants public recognition to different groups who are encouraged to retain their differences and will receive state support and recognition. This can take at least three forms: federal autonomy in the form of self-government (e.g. for French speakers, Aboriginal peoples), poly-ethnic rights for the various ethnic minorities, and special representation rights for various disadvantaged groups (Kymlicka, 1996). Thus all that is required is only a minimal commitment to the shared political culture of the public domain. India is also an example of constitutionally grounded multiculturalism designed to accommodate the major divisions within the state.

There is clearly a delicate balance between maintaining integration and divisiveness, as is strikingly evident in the case of Belgium and perhaps too in the case of India, or even secession as in the case of more overt expressions of nationalism such as in Ireland (O'Mahony and Delanty, 1998). The communitarian model is quite a departure from the American constitutional liberal model in that groups are encouraged to retain their cultural identity. It differs from the liberal model in that it recognizes that the neutrality of the state must be compromised in order to maximize inclusion on the social level. It differs furthermore from the American liberal model in that it does not believe that social integration will be achieved as a result of the mutual mixing of cultures. In short, the state must take an active role in bringing about social integration. This model of multiculturalism may be cast in the terms of the communitarian 'politics of recognition', to use Charles Taylor's characterization of what constitutes a multicultural society and which was discussed in Chapter 4 (Taylor, 1994). Taylor is opposed to the classic liberal stance (the model of assimilation) in that for him the state must recognize cultural identity, for political identity must rest on a particular cultural identity. What this translates into is a plea for collective rights for culturally defined groups. This stance is what makes communitarian multicultural distinctive, as well as highly controversial (Bauböck, 2000; Offe, 1998).

While the former models were products of an industrial society that was still shaped by Enlightenment civil society, the communitarian model is a product of the postindustrial society; it is an expression of a society in which immigrant groups can organize themselves in quasi-corporate orders and gain access to a form of political organization that is more regulatory than liberal in its fundamental assumptions. It may also be noted that this model is seen as concerned primarily with access to social and cultural citizenship. It has not been dominant in cases of political disputes concerning fundamental questions of group identity. In such cases the radical multicultural model has been more prevalent.

Liberal communitarian multiculturalism[3]

This is often to be found at the sub-national level and can co-exist with other more official kinds of multiculturalism. In many of its conceptions it is not essentially different from the previous model but may be distinguished from communitarianism in that it reflects a weaker form of multiculturalism. British multi-culturalism takes this liberal form which is one of pluralism, and derives from colonial history and the Commonwealth. The emphasis is on co-operation and peaceful co-existence rather than a formal policy of containment. It may be termed 'liberal communitarian' in that there is official recognition of diversity but measures stop short of positive programmes to empower groups. It is a liberalism that has been modified by communitarianism. Unlike the stronger Canadian model ethnic groups are not seen as being on an equal footing with the dominant cultural group in the society (for instance, it is generally assumed that immigrants will learn the language of the majority). The liberal component is strong in that there is tacit recognition of a dominant cultural group but within an ethos of tolerance. The metaphor of 'the salad bowl' rather than the 'melting-pot' captures best this kind of multiculturalism, which is one of the most prevalent traditions in western Europe and in much of the rest of the world. Such an understanding of multiculturalism has received a theoretical formulation in the recent work of Alain

Touraine who argues for a reconciliation of liberalism and communitarianism (Touraine, 2000). It is also the basis of Habermas' notion of multiculturalism within the limits of a 'constitutional patriotism' and Bhiku Parekh's equally dialogic theory of multiculturalism (Habermas, 1998; Parekh, 2000).

In this context there is also the question of the different status of immigrants and indigenous peoples, as Kymlicka argues (1995). Defending the application of group differentiated rights to indigenous, colonized peoples who have suffered a historical grievance, he questions its application to immigrant ethnic groups who have wilfully joined the society in order to benefit from it. In many countries, for instance the USA and Australia, liberal communitarianism has been used to justify self-government for indigenous peoples. In the UK, a form of devolution based on differential rights has been seen as the solution for Northern Ireland and for Scotland. However, liberal communitarism does not demand a wider conception of group rights. In sum, this model is largely a strategy to accommodate within a broadly liberal framework the reality of cultural diversity. It is supplementary rather than innovating and frequently indistinguishable from intercultural tokenism.

Interculturalism

This is a more recent soft kind of multiculturalism that seeks to promote cultural difference as a positive virtue (see Watson, 2000, p. 51). It is expressed in programmes of cultural awareness and seeks to encourage tolerance but also knowledge of other cultures. Most countries today have educational policies designed to promote cultural understanding. It is a kind of multiculturalism that has resonances in particular kinds of consumerism and in advertising.

POST-MULTICULTURALISM

In recent years, in particular since the mid-1980s, multiculturalism has taken a radical turn, in effect abandoning multiculturalism in a new politics of cultural difference. Whereas modern multiculturalism, as discussed in the previous section, sought to further the equality of all groups in society and to create a common political community, recent developments suggest a move towards difference as itself a goal to be achieved. The following are the main conceptions of what might be called post-multiculturalism: radical multiculturalism, critical multiculturalism, transnational multiculturalism.

Radical multiculturalism

This is the view that disadvantaged groups must be privileged in order to empower them against the dominant groups. In this more radical or 'strong' conception of multiculturalism, the state must intervene actively in granting recognition to marginal groups. This is the main form that multiculturalism takes in the USA today, where the melting-pot model, discussed above, has ceased to have any relevance. This is because the main issues today are framed in the language of race rather than of ethnicity. It is a question of making institutions more representative of their social environment rather than shaping a common way of life, or even accommodating cultural identity. The form it takes is that of affirmative action, since multiculturalism is now a matter of positive programmes, in particular in education and in jobs.

Unlike in Europe, where multiculturalism is addressed mostly to first and second generation immigrants and refugees, the American debate today is largely about the diversity of the society's native population (Glazer, 2000). It has found controversial expression in debates about the curriculum and has fuelled the culture wars in higher education (Delanty, 2001). It has been more divisive than integrative, in the view of many critics who believe that radical multiculturalism is racist in conception since its key element is the proposition of essential difference (exactly in contradiction with human rights philosophy which posits sameness or equality).

Critical multiculturalism

This idea of multiculturalism is close to the communitarian model discussed above, but is more radical in that it is ultimately a theory of cultural plurality that goes beyond all traditional understandings of multiculturalism (see Goldberg, 1994). It differs from radical multiculturalism in one respect: the groups in question are largely 'post-ethnic' – they can be found as much in the dominant cultural groups as in ethnic groups – and the state is expected to be proactive, as opposed to reactive, in promoting citizenship (Hollinger, 1995). For critical multiculturalism differences within ethnic groups are emphasized and ultimately it is a conception of multiculturalism that recognizes the pluralization of all group identities.

Iris Young's conception of a strong communitarianism fits into this model of group differentiated rights around issues of bilingual education, women's rights and rights for disadvantaged groups such as disabled people (Young, 1989; 1990; see also Guttman, 1993; O' Neill, 1994). Feminists and cultural pluralists who advocate group differentiated citizenship (Isin, 2000; see also Chapter 3) see identity as contested and therefore always open to definition.

The critical multiculturalism model highlights the conflict of collective rights for groups and individual rights, i.e. the right of the individual to dissent from the ethnic group. Thus the emphasis here is less on multiculturalism in the sense of cultures in the plural than of the pluralization of culture. It must be mentioned that this model is largely philosophical, with resonances in debates about postmodernization, and cannot be related so easily to particular kinds of policies (Delanty, 2000a).

Transnational multiculturalism

The emphasis here is on a more flexible kind of citizenship that is emerging with globalization and new kinds of governmentality. Especially in Southeast Asia, as Aihwa Ong has documented, the state is often willing to let corporate entities set the terms for regulating citizenship. The results, she claims, are different regimes of rights, discipline, caring and security (Ong, 1999). One consequence for citizenship is the need for dual and even multinationalities. However, the implications of this model for multiculturalism are unclear (see also Chapter 8 for further discussion on transnationalism and cosmopolitanism).

BEYOND MULTICULTURALISM? RECOVERING THE SOCIAL

At this point we have reached the limits of multiculturalism. In communitarian theories as well as the older liberal conceptions, group identity was taken for granted as something fixed and belonging either to the private domain or reducible to a public notion of the common good. Several models of multiculturalism discussed in this chapter are commonly regarded as unacceptable and are in fact contrary to international law (and may even entail severe violations of human rights if they are implemented). Some of the more recent models of multiculturalism suggest a move beyond some of the assumptions of these older models, which presuppose the national democratic state as the operative framework. Whether it is the constitution or the curriculum, multiculturalism has irreversibly politicized citizenship, albeit to the point of calling into question the very possibility of social integration. Given the reality of cultural diversity as a result of immigrant, ethnic, various subcultural and postmodernized identities, how much common ground is there in contemporary societies? What criteria do we use to define a community? Does multiculturalism sustain social integration or is it divisive?

Several developments must be commented on. There is no doubt that liberal or republican multiculturalism no longer caries any weight. The classical American model is now believed widely to be a failure, or politically exhausted, at least if we follow communitarian and liberal critiques (Lazare, 1996; Schlesinger, 1992). Many critics argue that assimilation has been possible only at the cost of ghettoization and new forms of social exclusion have emerged (Wacquant, 1993). However, this is not to deny the relative success of American multiculturalism, since there has been considerable assimilation and the term has been normalized (Glazer, 1997; see also Smelser and Alexander, 1999). What is apparent however is that this model may have reached its limits. A new multiculturalism has emerged – though whether or not this is as a result of the failure of assimilation is an open question – seeking to empower positively groups through collective rights and the re-politicization of cultural identity. The French republican model, which is also practised in Turkey where the state is officially secular, is unable to stem the rising tide of religion and ethnic identity, and may even encourage it insofar as it fails to create a space for different cultures. This model presupposes widespread secularism (and possibly even militarism). But one of the features of the current situation is the crisis of secularism. Pluralist multiculturalism has been more successful. As Soysal has argued, immigrants, at least within the countries of the European Union, have now extended their rights so far that they can challenge national governments by appealing directly to EU authorities (Soysal, 1994; see also Cesarani and Fulbrook, 1996). In the context of my argument concerning citizenship and multiculturalism, what this means is that multiculturalism has ceased to be a container for immigrants, but has become an expression of the diversity of contemporary society.[4] Culture and society can no longer be separated any more than politics can be separated from the social.

The boundaries between social groups are more diffuse than previously. The implication for multiculturalism is that it is more and more difficult to demarcate ethnic groups, and the boundary between ethnic groups and the majority culture is not always so clearly defined. This is not unconnected to the fact that today many immigrants are middle-class professionals (Ong, 1999). There is also the crucially important factor of consumption and the reality of much unrecognized social integration, as Steinberg has argued (Steinberg, 1989). This thesis that the new multiculturalism has derived precisely from the success of the earlier models has also been more recently polemically restated by Russell Jacoby who argues that a myth of cultural difference has been created by academics who have applied the curriculum debates and the 'all is culture' philosophy to society, thus distorting the reality of widespread integration (Jacoby, 1999). In the view of many there is the danger that multiculturalism is a form of cultural separation and also fails to solve the problem of reconciling tolerance of group differences with the need to allow individuals to dissent from the groups (Eisenberg, 1999).

The presuppositions of multicultural citizenship no longer exist. Migration is increasing worldwide at a time when the developed world is becoming more concerned with exclusionary policies to restrict entry. With over 120 million immigrants worldwide and over 20 million refugees, the nation-state is under pressure since the older model was not designed for such great numbers. As Sassen points out: 'Large-scale international migrations are highly conditioned and structured, embedded in complex economic, social, and ethnic networks. States may insist on treating immigration as the aggregate outcome of individual actions, but they cannot escape the consequences of those larger dynamics' (Sassen, 1996, p. 75; see also Sassen, 1999).

Western multiculturalism emerged on the basis of economic and social stability. Within the countries of the developed world multicultural citizenship has become unstable. Economic insecurity has risen, the welfare state is no longer able to absorb all kinds of social problems, and the cultural presuppositions of western multiculturalism have been undermined by rising nationalism and the emergence of second and third generation immigrants who no longer share the same commitments of the first generation and are becoming more integrated into mainstream society. Indeed, as Russell Jocoby argues, quoting Marcus Lee Hanson, claims about ethnic pluralism often derive from integrated immigrants who are reinventing the long-lost roots of their grandparents: 'what the son wishes to forget the grandson wishes to remember' (quoted in Jacoby, 1999, p. 48). Ironically then radical multiculturalism may be the product of assimilation, not its failure.

In sum, the size and status of immigrants has changed, undermining the established conceptions of multiculturalism. Moreover, it is increasingly difficult to say what is a cultural identity and what is a political identity. These are no longer separated in the way they once were as a result of pervasive de-differentiating processes. Along with the wider diffusion of the private and the public, cultural identities are becoming more hybrid and political identities are less separated from cultural identity. While many ethnic groups retain their language, this is not a marker of cultural separation. The dominant groups in society have themselves been transformed by ethnic multiculturalism. Today cultural diversity rests less on ethnic heterogeneity – the pluralism of 'cultural forms of life' – than on the emergence of new sub-cultures based on class, gender, religion and lifestyles shaped by consumption; that is, the ideology of ethnic diversity is no longer the basis of multiculturalism (Fischer, 1999). Underlying all these modes of social action is a pronounced individuation in identity and values. Consequently, it is no longer evident exactly what constitutes a cultural community.

CONCLUSION

Western multiculturalism rested on the assumption that diversity lay primarily on the level of cultural identity and that this was shaped largely by the ethnic values of relatively homogeneous groups of immigrants who were quite separate from the dominant, national society. If we have reached the limits of multiculturalism today it is because the assumption that ethnic groups are internally homogeneous and therefore distinct from the national community is no longer valid: cultural diversity has penetrated the heart of the cultural ethos of society and has diluted the distinction between a pre-political cultural identity and a neutral public culture that is the guarantee of the national community's identity. Multiculturalism today must reconcile itself to the reality of 'post-ethnicity' (Hollinger, 1995). In short, the 'ethos of pluralization', to use William Connolly's term (1995), has penetrated into the political domain transforming the relationship between state and society.

6

COMMUNITIES OF DISSENT
The idea of communication communities

A point has been reached in this book where community as communication must be discussed. Until now the main conceptions of community were those of classical sociological theory and political philosophy. In all of these there is a view of community as largely affirmative of the prevailing society. Mainstream, classical sociology stressed the integrative capacity of community, seeing community as a legitimation of the established society and of the identity of its members (although identity was not a concept familiar to the classical sociologists). In this tradition, community has been very centrally conceived in terms of tradition. Although there have been some important departures from this, as in Victor Turner's idea of the confluence of liminality and communitas, a post-traditional conception of community has not been accompanied by a view of community as transformative of society. This conservative view of community has also been reflected in the idea of community in political philosophy. In the

American tradition of communitarianism, community has been seen largely as appropriate to a modern urban society in its retreat from the social ills of modernity. However, despite this search for a modern kind of community that may be capable of offering an antidote to the malaise of modernity, communitarianism has reflected a very anti-political view of community. As noted in Chapter 2, in its civic republican formulations, it is a view of community that is very much disengaged from the state, locating community in the voluntaristic domain. Other versions of communitarianism stress the importance of the state to give some official status to particular cultural communities in order to foster a civic patriotism. This is clearly not a view of community as a basis of an alternative vision of society but an accommodation of groups within the larger framework.

This chapter addresses the radical dimension of community as expressed in protest, in the quest for an alternative society or the construction of collective identity in social movements. What is suggested by this conception of community as dissent is a more communicative model. Communities of dissent, or 'communities of resistance', are essentially communicative in their organization and composition, and in this they contrast with the emphasis on the symbolic, the civic and the normative in the other major models. In this sense of community, what is distinctive is not merely a normative vision of an alternative society, as in some of the great ideologies of modernity discussed in Chapter 1, but the construction of a communicative project that is formed in the dynamics of social action.

The chapter proceeds as follows. The first section looks at some critical theories of community (Habermas, Touraine and Bauman) and argues, following Habermas, for a notion of communication community. The second section discusses the connection between community and social movements. In this view community emerges out of the mobilization of people around a collective goal. In the third section, an attempt is made to reassess the idea of individualism. It is argued that the new interpretations of individualism, as in the work of Ulrich Beck and others, suggest that the dichotomy of community and individual must be abandoned.

CRITIQUES OF COMMUNITY: HABERMAS, TOURAINE AND BAUMAN

The social theories of Habermas, Touraine and Bauman are all marked by a distrust of the very idea of community. At this juncture in the book some consideration will be given to their critiques of community, which offer a perspective that is neither liberal nor communitarian. Habermas' and Touraine's critique of community is aimed largely at communitarianism and more generally at nationalism, while Bauman's critique of community is aimed at the nostalgia for community in contemporary society where the problem of insecurity has become acute.

Habermas' position on community is ambivalent. On the one side, he rejects some of the basic premises of communitarianism, in particular the tendency in communitarian thought to conceive of society as a moral totality, and, on the other side, he wants to retrieve the notion of a communication community, which is in danger of instrumentalization by commodified social relations. Communication as a form of social action is the central concept in his work (Habermas, 1984, 1987). Social action is based on language and, in this view, society is a linguistically created and sustained entity. For Habermas communication is open-ended and is the basis of all social action; it can never be reduced to an instrumental relationship since the communicative process always resists closure and thus ultimately resists domination. This transcendental component of communication means that it contains within it a degree of critique and reflexivity. The aim of Habermas' social theory of modernity is to uncover the communicative rationality in modern society and to demonstrate how communicative structures provide the basis of political possibilities. His theory of modernity thus aims to reconstruct modernity in terms of the expansion of critical forms of communication that are capable of resisting the other face of modernity, namely the instrumentalized forces of capitalism. More generally, this theorization of modern society is also one of a conflict of system and life-world whereby the communicative structures of the latter resist the instrumental rationality of the system.

Communication for Habermas operates on two levels. It is the basic medium of social integration and is the means of reconciling conflict, including competing political positions. On the first level, communication is embedded in the basic linguistic nature of social action. All social action is mediated by language and the essence of language is the social act of shared worlds. Although power relations and various pathologies disguise and distort communicative structures, it is always in principle possible that people, despite their differences, can agree on certain things. The very fact that social action is articulated through language implies the possibility of a shared conception of truth, justice, ethics and politics. The very capacity to speak entails an orientation to a possible agreement with another person and the tacit assumption of a shared world. Indeed, the very idea of the life-world is a communitarian notion. Although a consensus will never be arrived at, the capacity for people to deliberate in communicative modes of action can never be excluded in principle. This constitutes the second level of language, the reflective and critical dimension of deliberative communication, which is a point removed from, but always presupposed in, everyday life. In his study of the public sphere, Habermas argued how modern societies institutionalized spaces for public discourse (Habermas, 1989). His idea of discursive democracy reflects this basic communitarian understanding of politics as a dialogic process.

The ambivalence of community is that it can either be the expression of the communicative action of the life-world or it can be a retreat from communication in a purely moral stance that leaves the structure of domination untouched. As a communicative concept, then, community has been quite important in Habermas' social theory. The idea of a 'communication community' means that social relations in modern society are organized around communication rather than by other media such as authority, status or ritual. While of course power and money – along with law – are the most important media in steering modern society, it is a basic premise of Habermas' work that such systemic forms of reproduction always face resistance from the recalcitrant life-world which is reproduced by different logics and which are inextricably linked with communication. In modern society, there are more and more communicative spaces, the most significant being the public sphere and science. The public sphere consists of a multiplicity of communicative sites, which can exist at all levels of society ranging from nationally specific forms of civil society to transnational discourses.[1] Science and the institution of the modern university, too, is an open communication community, according to Habermas, since it is characterized by a commitment to truth that can in principle be settled only by consensus.[2] The notion that truth can be arrived at only in a deliberative manner and settled by consensus is the kernel of Habermas' theory of communication. It is this idea that leads him to reject communitarianism and to look to an alternative and more communicative idea of community. If community is what is shared, this must take a communicative form. This is the implication of Habermas' theory of communicative action. It also points to a transformative idea of community as the bringing to expression of communicative competences. Community is never complete but is always emergent.

For Habermas, communitarians such as, for instance, Charles Taylor or Hannah Arendt reduce the social to a moral totality rather than see it as a communicative structured process that is always in tension with the existing society. In fact, communitarianism ignores the communicative dimension of community, seeing it instead as merely moral or civic. For Habermas this reductive and highly normative stance in communitarianism denies the transformative moment in modern society, which derives from the very structures of communication. His critique of communitarianism does not share the liberal position, since the point is not the loss of moral individualism but the denial of the critical reflective capacity of society.[3] In fact, Habermas shares with communitarians the desire to go beyond liberalism's moral individualism but does not agree with their commitment to an underlying morality. The morality of a community not only lays down how its members should act: it also provides grounds for the consensual resolutions of relevant conflicts (Habermas, 1998, p. 4). His position, especially in his recent work, stresses the existence of multiple communication communities and, in his more recent works, a multi-dimensional view of political community as also existing at the level of global society.

While Habermas' critique of communitarism has been shaped by his support for European integration and the recognition that cosmopolitan forms of community are becoming more and more important today, he is also responding to the dangers that community has represented in the context of Germany. Community has been one of the major legitimations of nationalism and in the extreme case it has provided a justification for fascism. As a moral totality, community is a dangerous sentiment since it reduces society to a non-social principle and it binds modernity to a premodern conception of society. For all these reasons, his social theory is very uneasy with the term community, although he never explicitly rejects it. Indeed, the very assumptions of his theory of communicative action presuppose the social and cultural context of a shared life-world. Shifting the focus from community to communication solves some of the difficulties with which community is beset. In this sense, then, the idea of community as communication community recalls the more variable and fluid notion of communitas discussed above.

This critical position on community is also found in Alain Touraine's work on democracy and modernity. Community and nationalism are very close, he argues. One of the most common expressions of community is *völkisch* sentiment and the notion that society is based on a pre-established unity over and above the individual and all social groups whose diversity must be denied in the assertion of wholeness. Touraine sees as the main challenge to democracy conceptions of politics that appeal to cultural heritage, community and nationalism. This does not mean that he is opposed to community in the sense of collective goals or the common good. The problem is that community has been debased by nationalism: 'Has not the pursuit of the common good become an obsession with identity and do we not need stronger institutional guarantees of respect for personal liberty and human rights rather than more integrated communities?' (Touraine, 1997, p. 112; see also pp. 65–8 and Touraine, 2000).

His theory of modernity sees society today as divided between a struggle of community versus markets and individualism (Touraine, 1995). In this situation, democracy is denied a social space, since it can exist in neither markets nor in community. A world dominated by community seeks only integration, homogeneity and consensus, rejecting democratic debate: 'A communitarian society is suffocating and can be transformed into a theocratic or nationalist despotism', he argues, and something like a 'cultural totalitarianism' is emerging today with community being resurrected by authoritarian forms of religion (Touraine, 1995, pp. 304, 311–12).

In contrast to community democracy allows a society to be both united and at the same time divided in the sense of a pluralist democracy consisting of many voices. However, this is not to say that Touraine is opposed to the principle of unity, which is in fact quite central to his thought. It might be suggested that like Habermas he is looking for an alternative conception of political community that does not reduce community to an underlying unity but builds upon diversity and communicative possibilities. Community alone will not achieve unity, according to Touraine, who is looking for a contemporary equivalent to the great social movements of modernity. The problem with community is that it places too much weight on identity: 'A society which defines itself primarily in terms of its identity cannot be democratic. Still less a society which defines itself in terms of its uniqueness. Such a society is too caught up in a logic that benefits only the State, which then reduces society to the nation and the multiplicity of social actors to the unity of the people' (Touraine, 1995, p. 343). Identity is central to community and to social movements, but when it becomes the sole component of a movement the result can only be an excessive preoccupation with the self and political impotence.

Zygmunt Bauman shares with Touraine and Habermas a deep scepticism of community. Community promises security but delivers only nostalgia and illusion, he argues in a recent book on community. It is, he says, merely a word that conveys a feeling of security that makes the world a warm and cosy place: 'We miss community because we miss security, a quality crucial to a happy life, but one which the world we inhabit is ever less able to offer and ever more reluctant to promise' (Bauman, 2001a, p. 144). It is also a place where nobody is a stranger and where there is a shared understanding of society. However, it comes at a price, for security and freedom do not fit too easily together. In a true community there is no criticism or opposition. But this community does not exist as a natural entity, except perhaps as a utopia. The really existing community is a besieged fortress defending itself against the outside world. Bauman sees the contemporary world as one obsessed with digging cultural trenches. In fact, community is being resurrected today as the problem of identity becomes more acute. As real communities decline, identity replaces it around a new understanding of community. As a surrogate for community, it has reinvented identity (Bauman,

2001a, p. 15). This is a point Eric Hobsbawm has made in *The Age of Extremes*: 'Never was the word "community" used more indiscriminately and emptily than in the decades when communities in the sociological sense became hard to find in real life' (Hobsbawm, 1994, p. 428).

The problem is that community is impossible because it cannot solve the problems with which it is confronted, in particular the problem of moral choice and uncertainty. Rather than facing these challenges directly, community offers only a comfortable illusion. In this sense, then, community was never lost – it was never born. Community is constantly appealed to by a present, dissatisfied with itself and needing the illusion of an alternative whether redeemed from the past or the promise of a utopia.

Communitarian thought, he argues, merely uncritically takes over the discourse of community and thereby simplifies greatly the social and existential problems of insecurity. Bauman shares with Habermas and Touraine a belief that something resembling community is possible but it needs to be redeemed from communitarianism and nationalism. 'If there is to be a community in the world of individuals, it can only be (and needs to be) a community woven together from sharing and mutual care; a community of concern and responsibility for the equal right to be human and the equal ability to act on that right' (Bauman, 2001a, pp. 149–50). Against community and its false promises, Bauman argues for a postmodern ethics based on individual autonomy and in which the exclusion of the other is not the price to be paid for the identity of the self. Such a postmodern ethics cannot hide from the fact of insecurity but must live up to it.

In sum, the critical approaches to community in the work of Habermas, Touraine and Bauman might urge us to abandon community altogether. It would appear that community is not entirely compatible with a conception of modernity that stresses the critical power of communication and reflexivity. However, much of the problem with community can be resolved by taking a communicative approach to it. In this respect Habermas' notion of a communicatively constituted community offers an alternative to Bauman's stronger ethical position. The idea of a communication community can be theorized in a way that lends itself to a world of multiple belongings and one in which integration is achieved more by communication than by an already existing morality and consensus. In this context social movement theory – with its themes of dissent and identity as practice – has much to offer such a theory of community as communication.

COMMUNITY, SOCIAL MOVEMENTS AND THE POLITICS OF IDENTITY

The growing literature on new social movements offers a quite different perspective on community than in communitarian thought. One of the main ideas in communitarianism as a sociological theory about modern urban society was the view that individualism is detrimental to community and that the decline in community, as measured in civic pride, social capital, voluntarism, is as a result of the pervasive spread of individualism. This view has been challenged by social movement research, which presents a very different understanding of the relationship between community and individualism. Research on new social movements reveals that individualism is in fact the basis of a good deal of communal activity and that what sustains many kinds of collective action is precisely strong individualism. Commitment to a communal cause of a collective goal rests on individualism which cannot be reduced to egoistic self-interest or to a non-social concept of the person. Personal self-fulfilment and individualized expression can be highly compatible with collective participation. For instance, educated people, who have a relatively high degree of personal autonomy, are attracted to collective action in order to realize their creativity and desire for recognition which may be blocked in other areas, such as in work and family life. Community can be a means of releasing the cultural creativity that late modernity produces but does not fully exploit.

According to Paul Lichterman in a study on commitment and community, widespread dedication to personal fulfilment is a cultural accomplishment. In other words, participation in community life can reinforce the quest for personal achievement. Personalist ways of creating community may be found in all kinds of community organization and groups, from small self-help groups to religious groups and grass-roots political groups. This confluence of individualism as personalism and community has resonances in much of communitarianism, but ultimately points towards a more open and democratic kind of community as communication. Communitarians tend to see personalism as decadent and corrosive of community. As Lichterman says, 'Communitarians focus less on what communities can do for individuals and more on what members do to maintain a community' (Lichterman, 1996, p.10). He opposes the 'see-saw' image of self-expression and private life pulling down public virtue, civic engagement and morality. We do not always choose between personal gratification and service to a common cause, he argues. The image of the see-saw highlights the tendency in communitarianism to stress dichotomous distinctions between the individual and the community and to believe that these polar opposites must be balanced in some way. Against this way of thinking he argues for a rethinking of individualism itself, especially in order to understand the kinds of commitment that lie behind radical democratic politics. For example, the culture of individualism and personal autonomy is something that has been the basis of Green politics in many countries and has been expressed in a sense of public responsibility that comes from a collective commitment and the valuing of each person's contribution. Insofar as it can lead to empowerment, community can reinforce personalism, giving to the individual a stronger sense of identity.

In bringing expressivist individualism into the picture Lichterman has struck a major blow against moral individualism as the exclusive kind of individualism. While communitarians have generally defined their stance as one opposed to the alleged moral individualism of liberalism, radical politics points to another kind of individualism. In this view of community, people from diverse backgrounds can come together in communal activism united by a common commitment and the solidarity that results. Expressivist individualism is a cultural phenomenon that had its roots in the counter-culture of the 1960s and 1970s and which became adopted to the more mainstream society of middle-class consumption in the 1980s. While some critics – Christopher Lasch, for example – have called this the return to the self, the minimal self, cultural narcissism and cynicism, others, for instance Melucci, Beck and Giddens, have seen in it the basis of a personalized or an individuated politics based on reflexivity and autonomy.

Alberto Melucci is the theorist who has most persuasively written on how self-realization has been enhanced by participation in collective action which in the new social movement is not based on the same separation of private and public that was characteristic of the labour movement. Individuated personal life is the basis of participation in collective action today, he argues, and what gets produced and reappropriated in the new politics is meaning. With the declining significance of the older social movements – the suffragette movement, the labour movements, trade unions and social democracy – and the rise of new social movements and counter-movements that are not organized primarly in the state and draw their support from class struggles, politics has become more centrally defined around the self and identity. Many of the new social movements – feminism, the peace movement, the ecological movement, gay rights movements, quality of life movements, anti-globalization movements – have made collective identity central to their politics and, where this has not been explicitly the case, many movements owe their influence to their ability to create powerful collective identities. In any case, whether the movement is primarily about identity politics, collective identities have either been the beginning or more commonly the outcome of many of the new social movements. This undoubtedly also applies to the examples more typically found in communitarian literature, such as self-help organizations, civic voluntarism and various kinds of local organization. To the extent that collective identity is involved, this is not necessarily the basis but the outcome of community. But here again, what is really the issue is community as action. Melucci argues that the 'collective action of many recent social movements constitutes a communicative act which is performed through the form of action itself, making visible new powers and the possibilities of challenging them' (Melucci, 1996a, p. 79).

What is suggested by the notion of community in social movement research is that community is something constructed; it is not an already existing set of values that are essential for social integration and the identity of the individual.[4] Community is not an underlying reality but is constructed in actual processes of mobilization. It is a processal concept of community in which community is defined and constructed in social action rather than residing in values and normative structures. Neither identity nor community, if we follow Melucci, can be treated as a reality or a 'thing' that can be related to an underlying subject, structure or system of values. Instead such constructs must be seen as a system of relations and one that is sustained by action rather than by culture, which is merely the outcome of action. Identity is not a resource for community that may be drawn upon, as might also be suggested by the idea of community as symbolically constructed. It is more than a question of the symbolic affirmation of an existing community because what is constructed is often an alternative society. Community is not a static notion, but is defined in the achieving of it. In this sense, then, community has a cognitive function in imagining and instituting a new kind of society. As discussed in Chapter 1, this radical impulse has always been present in the idea of community which has often been a quest for a new age. However, what is different about the idea of community implicit in the politics of the new social movements is that the search for an alternative society is connected with everyday life and the mobilization of the resources of the life-world. In breaking down the distinction between private and public and in politicizing the community of reference, a culturally radical concept of community comes into play in reshaping the political field.

This way of looking at community also brings the debate beyond the idea of community as sub-cultures that seek an alternative to the status quo. Sub-cultures were based on the radicalization of style and the subversion of meaning, which managed to sustain a community of opposition for the youth culture. While sub-cultures sought a certain subversion of the status quo on the level of culture, the New Age communities of recent times offer a non-political conception of community to their followers. With their roots in the self-expressivist culture that emerged in the 1960s, New Age movements have not brought about widespread social transformation. In the past few decades there has been an explosion in the number of spiritual movements, ranging from pagan and occult movements to religious communities, and numerous New Age movements that all proclaim some kind of alternative community. They are 'anti-political' in their exclusive concern with subjectivity and identity (see the discussion on postmodern community in Chapter 7). The new social movements discussed above differ from them in their stronger focus on collective politics and the desire to bring about social transformation. For this reason we can say that commitment rather than merely personal fulfilment is central to the new social movements. It may also be remarked that the new social movements are, as the term suggests, 'social' movements as opposed to cultural movements, or political movements in the narrow sense of politics. Their objective, which is central to their identity, is social transformation and it is for this reason that the personal politics that sustains them ultimately goes beyond individualism in the pursuit of a collective goal.

INDIVIDUALISM RECONSIDERED

Given the centrality of the concept of individualism in debates about community, some consideration of the different notions of individualism is warranted. As is clear from the above discussion, there is as little clarity on the meaning of the word *individualism* – which is one of the most widely used terms in social and political science – as there is of the word *community*. We are supposed to be living in an age of individualism, and modern political theory has made the individual the measure of all political systems, but when we look more closely at this word we find that it is highly contested. Building upon the discussion on community and social movements in the preceding section, the following is an attempt to summarize the main conceptions of individualism that predominate today in the social and political literature. It is by no means a complete list of all uses of the term. The argument that emerges from this is a view of individualism that goes beyond moral individualism and is compatible with community.

Moral individualism

This is the mainstream liberal concept of the person and is also the basis of much of rational choice theory and methodological individualism. In this view the individual is an autonomous and rational agent. Moral individualism is conceived essentially in terms of the individual as a pre-social being and as a responsible agent. Moral individualism holds that the individual is the measure of all things and is a free agent, and therefore responsible for his or her actions. This notion of individualism has often been associated with market individualism, or what C.P. MacPherson has called 'possessive individualism'; that is, an individualism defined in terms of ownership of property (MacPherson, 1962). Moral individualism in this sense is an ideology of the market society and thus reflects a bourgeois notion of the individual as a free agent. It has been the basis of some of the most influential ideas of the modern age, such as the idea of self-determination. It has been strongly opposed to all kinds of collectivism, and in more recent times it has enjoyed a renaissance with rational choice theory.[5]

Collective individualism

In opposition to the liberal concept of moral individualism, communitarian authors such as Charles Taylor have stressed the social nature of the individual as one that is quite literally embodied in moral relationships (Taylor, 1990). This concept of the self suggests a more sociological understanding of the individual than in liberal thinking. While its critics have often charged the notion of the self as social with an 'over-socialized' concept of the individual (Wrong, 1961), this cannot be too easily said of Taylor's theory of the self. Taylor follows Hegel in seeing the self as rooted in *Sittlichkeit*, an ethical community as opposed to the abstract and universalistic *Moralität* (Taylor, 1975, p. 376). The individual must be seen as rooted in the collective self. This position, discussed under communitarianism in Chapter 4, may be cited as the first major reconceptualization of the individual as shaped in community.

Autonomy of the self

Another tradition in modern thought emphasizes the less collective or socialized nature of the individual than the autonomy of the self (Honneth, 1995). In this way of looking at the individual the autonomy of the self is not compromised by socialization processes. Proponents of this conception of the self are represented strongly in the American tradition of pragmatism, as, for example, in the work of William James, and in symbolic interaction, as in the work of Charles Herbert Mead (see Joas, 1998). In this tradition, individualism is a social creation in the context of an intersubjective relation of self and other. This attempt to reconcile the moral autonomy of the self with the social context is very well illustrated in Castoriadis' theory of the self for whom moral autonomy is not achieved through repression but through an open relationship with the social world (Castoriadis, 1987).

Expressivist individualism

With its origins in romanticist thought and late nineteenth-century *Lebensphilosophie*, an expressivist concept of the individual came into prominence in the counter-culture of the latter part of the twentieth century. This understanding of the individual is quite different from the dominant traditions of moral and collective individualism. Expressivist individualism entails a view of the individual as dynamic and creative. Several critics have attacked this kind of individualism as one excessively concerned with a privatistic and inward self that is sustained by consumption and therapy. 'The therapeutic self', 'the narcissistic self' or 'the minimal self' are some of the designations of expressivist individualism (Lasch, 1979). Rejecting collective, public values for private ones, expressivist individualism is an anti-political individualism.

Individuation

Anthony Giddens argues that in late modern societies a new kind of individualism has been created whereby the self has become considerably empowered, although not necessarily emancipated (Giddens, 1990, 1991). The self has become more and more self-reflexive in the sense that the identity of the individual is constituted in increased 'self-monitoring' and 'self-control'. It is a view of the individual as one who can shape his or her own life project. Ulrich Beck also advocates this view of individualism as 'individualization' (Beck, 1997, 1998; Beck and Beck-Gernsheim, 2002). This does not mean simply freedom as an individual fate but a social fate. It may also mean more anxiety and insecurities (Pahl, 1995). Individuation is a product of the breakup of traditional roles and the organization of society around the individual who is becoming increasingly cut off from collective ties. The contemporary culture is an individualized one, argue Beck and Giddens. The concept of individualism is also present in the social theory of Zygmunt Bauman, who writes of 'individualized society' (Bauman, 2001b). In this kind of society there is more and more choice and the individual is constantly having to make choices of all kinds.

Personalism

As discussed earlier in this chapter, individualism may also be conceived in terms of what might be called *personalism*. This idea is implicit in the notion of individuation in Beck, Bauman and Giddens. However, while these authors refer mostly to the individual as the reference point, new social movement theory focuses on the collective actor and, as in the case of Melucci, there is a stronger emphasis on the social nature of the individual:

> As social processes in today's society have increasingly shifted their centre towards the individual, a kind of subjectivization and

interiorization of identity have taken place as a result. Yet this does not transform identity into a psychological construct, at least not in the reductive sense with which the term is often used. The construction of identity today involves our inner being for reasons that are profoundly social. Identity can be negotiated because there exists subjects of action who are no longer externally or objectively defined, but who themselves possess the capacity to produce and define the meaning of what they do.

(Melucci, 1996b, pp. 49–50)

The key characteristics of individualism as personalism are self-fulfilment, commitment, solidarity and collective responsibility (see also Lichterman (1996) and above). Personalism differs from expressivist individualism in that the self is shaped in participation in community and is sustained by a belief in collective goods. Thus, in this view, the cultural trend towards subjectivity is realized in a new kind of politics.

In view of these different concepts of individualism, we can no longer see community as something opposed to the individual. Social theory has moved beyond a dichotomous view of the individual and society as locked in conflict where a gain in one is the loss of the other. Thus in collective action the self is enhanced in its identity. As Della Porta and Diani (1999) argue, participants in social movements evolve their identity as a result of participating in collective action, suggesting that individualism can be collectively generated and also that community can be shaped by conflict.

CONCLUSION

The argument in this chapter has been that as a result of changed relations between society and the individual a space for community has emerged. This is most evident in the case of social movements and collective struggles. The understanding of community that this suggests is a constructivist one that emphasizes community as defined by practices rather than by structures or cultural values. Contemporary communities are groupings that are more and more wilfully constructed: they are products of 'practices' rather than of 'structures'. Communities are created rather than reproduced. Following Bourdieu (1990), we can say that community is a set a practices that constitute belonging. What is distinctive about these practices – and this is to move beyond Bourdieu – is that they are essentially reproduced in communication. In this sense we are also moving beyond the idea of symbolic community, since community is more than simply a resource of meaning and one animated by boundary distinctions. Communication communities are not shaped only by relations between insiders and outsiders, but by expansion in the community of reference and the construction of discourses of meaning.[6] Thus rather than being sustained by symbolic boundaries and a stable community of reference, communication communities are open horizons. This notion of the openness of community brings us to the question of post-modern community, the theme of Chapter 7.

7

POSTMODERN COMMUNITY
Community beyond unity

The idea that we are living in a postmodern society has been a topic much discussed in recent times. In the postmodern society group membership is more fluid and porous than in modern society. The old certainties of class, race, nation and gender that were the basis of the kind of society that emerged with industrialization have become contested categories in what is now an age of multiple belongings. But the postmodern age is also an insecure age which, in calling into question the assumptions of modernity, has made the problem of belonging more and more acute. The quest for belonging has occurred precisely because insecurity has become the main experience for many people. Even the very notion of society has been called into question, along with all kinds of fixed reference points and stable identities. Inevitably this questioning of previously held assumptions has also had implications for the idea of community, which has suffered the same fate as the societal discourses of nation, class, gender and race. The experience of contingency has entered into the very category of community itself, but this has not led to a decline in community. For some it has meant a crisis, and one that began with the recognition of 'community without propinquity' in post-Chicago urban sociology (see Chapter 3). But it is possible to see this situation as less one of crisis than one of renewal in which a new kind of community, one we may call postmodern community, is emerging. The characteristic of this is a shift from identity to difference, from certainty to contingency, a community beyond unity, from closed to open communities, and an embracing of liminality, which is to be found less on the margins of society than in its urban centres.

Postmodern community is to be found in a re-enchantment of everyday life and no longer on the margins of society, for in postmodern society marginality is everywhere. Postmodern communities are nomadic, highly mobile, emotional and communicative. These communication communities are sustained by mass culture and aesthetic sensibilities and practices rather than in symbolic battles between self and other. Postmodern community is a 'fractured community' that emerges along with the creation of non-foundational, heterogeneous societies (Lindroos, 2001). As something experienced in everyday life, it is not always a symbolic whole, as Schefer-Huges (1992) has shown. In the following discussion of postmodern community, after an initial look at some general conceptions of postmodernism, I discuss some postmodern theories of community. The third section focuses the debate on liminality and the postmodernization of everyday life, discussing some examples, such as taste communities, personal communities based on friendship and New Age travellers.

POSTMODERNITY AND THE REDISCOVERY OF
THE SELF

One of the major themes in postmodernist thought over the past twenty years concerns the identity of the self. The question Who am I? has returned today in a whole variety of contexts: in feminism, in multiculturalism, in ethnicity and in race. That it has become central to postmodernism is at first surprising, given that an older generation of thinkers associated with postmodernism – the post-structuralist generation represented by Michel Foucault – attempted to bury this question and with it even the very notion of the self. On closer inspection this is less surprising, for today the self has been liberated from many of the moulds against which these thinkers rebelled. The self is less trapped in the social institutions inherited from the nineteenth century and new kinds of struggle have appeared in which self and identity are often what the struggle is about. Strangeness has become more central to the self today, both in terms of a strangeness *within* the self and in the relationship *between* self and other. This experience of strangeness captures the essence of the postmodern sensibility, namely the feeling of insecurity, contingency and uncertainty both in the world and in the identity of the self.

Where modernist thought stressed the unity and coherence of the self, postmodernism emphasizes multiplicity and, above all, difference, for within every self is another self (Critchley, 1998). Where modernity found uniformity and equivalence, the post-modern turn found a plurality of fractured selves. In the work of figures such as Foucault, Lacan, Derrida, Deleuze and Guattari the self was revealed to be a constructed category and in some formulations was held to be schizophrenic (Elliott, 1999). Consequently the aim was simply to deconstruct the self without putting anything in its place. These conceptions of the self were of course influenced by the linguistic turn in modern thought which led to a view of everything being shaped by language and thus open to multiple readings. For Foucault, for instance, the self is created in discourses of power which are 'disciplinary'. More recent postmodern thought, under the influence of feminism, has somewhat changed the postmodern agenda whereby some of the extreme positions have been revised. This move is inspired by a recovery of the subject and is evident in the widespread concern with identity today. The old deconstructive movement, as associated with the largely French post-structuralist movements – Derrida, Barthes, Foucault, Lacan – was in fact hostile to the very idea of identity and aimed instead to get rid of the centrality of self and all aspirations for belonging. All claims about identity were dismissed as a quest for a false totality, a hankering after a founding origin or the illusion that history is based on some kind of meaningful narrative or founding subject. The idea of 'difference' suggested a conception of identity as always formed in opposition to something which is never explicit because it must be denied, but is none the less always present as a defining structure, the result being according to this view that the self is never fully coherent; it must suppress a part of itself. For Derrida, this in fact means that the self ultimately depends on the denial of the other.

However, in recent years even these post-structuralists have returned to the self, seeing new possibilities for a recovery of the human subject. The demise of the subject has not meant the death of the self. For instance, in his final writings Foucault became more interested in the possibility of a new ethics, and the recent work of Derrida reveals an interest in politics, friendship and a recovery of the social. Feminism, influenced heavily by deconstruction, has been particularly important in this regard, since the aim of feminism is not merely to deconstruct patriarchal identities but to define a feminist politics. Post-colonialism has also put the self, identity and belonging on the agenda (Spivak, 1987). These deconstructive approaches also have a constructive moment, for the aim is to give voice to marginalized people whose self-identity cannot be separated from their marginality. Political struggles begin thus with 'subaltern voices', according to theorists such as Spivak and Gilroy.

In sum, we can say that identity becomes an issue when the self ceases to be taken for granted. That is why modern thought did not make identity central (Wagner, 2001, pp. 66–9). The classical sociologists, for instance, did not go beyond the idea that the self, which is based on a degree of autonomy, is socially constructed. Thus they accepted both autonomy and domination as two sides to modern society. Today, identity has become an issue because the reference points for the self have become unstuck: the capacity for autonomy is no longer held in check by rigid structures, such as class, gender, nation, ethnicity. The self can be invented in many ways. The contemporary understanding of the self is that of a social self formed in relations of difference rather than of unity and coherence. Identity becomes a problem when the self is constituted in the recognition of difference rather than in sameness.

THE POSTMODERN THEORY OF COMMUNITY

In this section we look at some of the main applications of postmodernism to community. While some of this is abstract, the following section will attempt to relate these ideas to some concrete examples of postmodern community. The debate about community in a postmodern key revolves around the work of two French philosophers, Jean-Luc Nancy's *The Inoperative Community* (Nancy, 1991) and Maurice Blanchot's *The Unavowable Community* (Blanchot, 1988).[1] Both of these essays are in fact a dialogue with an earlier work by the enigmatic French thinker Georges Bataille, who has exhibited a certain fascination for Nancy and Blanchot. Other major works on postmodern community in this tradition of deconstructionism[2] are William Corlett's *Community without Unity* (Corlett, 1989), Giorgio Agamben's *The Coming Community*

(Agamben, 1993) and Michel Maffesoli's *The Time of the Tribes* (Maffesoli, 1996a).

The central idea of postmodern community for Blanchot and Nancy is that community is something experienced as a loss and therefore as an absence in people's lives. As Nancy says in the Preface his question is: 'how can the community without essence (the community that is neither "people" nor "nation", neither "destiny" nor "generic humanity," etc) be presented as such?' (Nancy, 1991, pp. xxxix–xl). Unlike nostalgic pleas for the recovery of community, these conceptions see community as impossible to realize. Community is experienced only as an absence which can be desired but never fulfilled. Community is the experience of a loss but not a loss of something that was once possessed. Inspired by Bataille, Nancy and Blanchot play with the idea that community is akin to experience of the death of a friend. It is this kind of loss that they speak of, but with the added sense that it is also the discovery of something that was never possessed and which can never be had. An example of this expression of community in the contemplation of death might be the widespread mourning that followed the death of Princess Diana in 1997. A community of mourning emerged around a cultural icon which had a purely imaginary dimension, as opposed to a normative one.

The notion of community that is expressed in their works is a communicative one. Greg Urban writes of community existing only in discourse (Urban, 1996). 'Community is what takes place through others and for others', writes Nancy (1991, p. 15). In community the self finds its identity in a relationship with others. This view of community resists every attempt to pin it down in an institutional or spatial structure, since it is something that is only experienced. For this reason, too, community is 'inoperative'; it can never be instrumentalized or institutionalized. The point is that community is experienced in a communicative relationship and not in a common bond as such, since it does not take a concrete form. 'Communication is not a bond', says Nancy (1991, p. 29). He thus speaks of a 'community without essence' to express this sense of community beyond consensus. He insists: 'we should become suspicious of the retrospective consciousness of the lost community and its identity (whether this consciousness conceives itself as effectively retrospective or whether, disregarding the realities of the past, it constructs images of this past for the sake of an ideal or a prospective vision)' (Nancy, 1991, p. 10). Such nostalgic images of the past have always existed.

> Society was not built on the ruins of a community. It emerged from the disappearance or the conservation of something – tribes or empires – perhaps just as unrelated to what we call 'community' as to what we call 'society'. So that community, far from being what society has crushed or lost, is what happens to us – question, waiting, event, imperative – in the wake of society.
>
> (Nancy, 1991, p. 11)

For Blanchot, community derives from the experience of friendship but can never be actualized, since it is always interrupted, broken or destroyed in some way. Hence the title of this original essay, 'The Negative Community'. Blanchot was fascinated by marginal and esoteric groups, such as gnostic and Christian sects, which were secretive and sought to subvert the social order. For Blanchot community expresses the incompleteness of society, the knowledge that society cannot realize the promise of a community to come. The assumption seems to be that community involves an intensity of experience that cannot be sustained by society. This seems to be indicated by the notion that community is 'negative', but the kind of community Blanchot speaks of is an 'elective community' which, unlike the traditional community, is chosen (Blanchot, 1988, pp. 46–7).

The suggestion, then, is that community expresses freedom, and that this consists of a withdrawal from society and even the transgression of limits.

William Corlett (1989), in applying Derrida's philosophy to community, argues that one expression of community is in the experience of difference. Derrida offers a radically new insight on community that goes beyond all traditional concepts. It is a view of community that consists of the mutual appreciation of differences and in which all oppositions are broken down. For Corlett, community may be mobilized to oppose oppression by displacing the centrality of the self. This is the lesson that Foucault and Derrida have taught, he argues. These thinkers have opposed the centrality of subjectivity and open community to something that is neither individualism nor collectivity but is based on sharing. In this he aims to go beyond communitarian political theory, which reproduces this dualism. While much of the argument about postmodern community is obscure, one important insight is that community may be conceived of as being beyond unity. Although no concrete examples are given in what is an explicitly philosophical discussion, it is possible to relate this idea of community to some contemporary experiences. In this regard one might mention what Bill Readings has called the 'community of dissensus'; that is, a kind of community that is not based on a common subjectivity, a collective 'we', or an underlying cultural identity (Readings, 1996, pp. 185–93).[3] This sense of community as an open communication community is expressed in certain kinds of experience of togetherness that can only be incomplete. What is characteristic of these experiences is the alterity of the self and other and the absence of a foundational reference point.

Scott Lash has also been influenced by Nancy. In his interpretation of postmodern community, community is conceptualized as reflexive, thus making a crucial link with an important strand in contemporary social theory. Lash, drawing also from Heidegger, emphasizes the shared nature of community, but not in the sense of traditional communities. Community today is more likely to be chosen and is therefore more reflexive. In this, Lash appropriates an idea central to the sociological theory of Pierre Bourdieu: reflexivity as the conscious questioning of social belonging. Reflexive communities have three aspects: 'first one is not born or "thrown", but "throws oneself" into them, second, they may be widely stretched over "abstract" space, and also perhaps over time; third, they consciously pose themselves the problem of their own creation, and constant re-invention far more than do traditional communities; fourth, their "tools" and products tend to be not material ones but abstract and cultural' (Lash, 1994, p. 161; see also Lash, 2002, pp. 20–37). The point, then, is that one important dimension of community today is its reflexive composition. For this reason Lash emphasizes the aesthetic sphere as the main location of reflexive community where a kind of 'groundless community' exists.

In order to prepare the way for a more sociological understanding of postmodern community, the work of Michel Maffesoli should be considered. In two of his works Maffesoli has written about the emergence of 'emotional communities' in the context of cultural transformation of contemporary society (Maffesoli, 1996a, 1996b). These emotional communities are marked more by an aesthetic sensibility than by symbolic codes. These 'tribes' of postmodernity's poly-culture are transgressive and insubstantial, even anomic: 'the emotional community is unstable, open, which may render it in many ways anomic with respect to the established moral order' (Maffesoli, 1996a, p. 15). They may be found in a proximity without space, in de-territorial groupings, in open networks. Emotional community is characterized 'by fluidity, occasional gatherings and dispersal' (Maffesoli, 1996a, p. 76). What he has in mind are new sects, possibly the occult, in which community is established in the attempt to 're-enchant the world'. Such expressions of community have a 'secretive' dimension, such as the Mafia, which is 'a metaphor of society' (Maffesoli, 1996a, p. 119). Thus he speaks of 'collective effervescence' – applying Durkheim's concept to the contemporary cultural context[4] – to refer to postmodern forms of community, which he calls 'tribes'. However, his concept of community differs from Durkheim's, who was concerned with the creation of modern forms of community suitable for large-scale societies and which might offer a civic morality. Maffesoli, on the contrary, is interested in quasi-religious sect-like movements that are secretive, vitalistic and highly emotional, and which arise out of 'tribes' rather than from 'masses'. In this sense he is closer to Simmel's theory of culture, which emphasized small groups and forms of cultural interaction that were not class specific, and to Victor Turner's theory of liminality and communitas, discussed in Chapter 2. However, Maffesoli sees mass society in decline – which rested on class-specific forms of consumption – and as being replaced by more heterogeneous forms of consumption and sociality based on new dynamics of group formation. With the 'tribalization' of the masses, culture has been fragmented and new kinds of community are emerging. In this respect he is also far from Turner's notion of a strong communitas binding a community together. As the subtitle of his book indicates, he also sees individualism in decline since these new tribes are products of neither individualism nor society.

The suggestion is that postmodern community is to be found in forms of sociation sustained by everyday life, in forms of consumption and in informal friendship networks (Maffesoli, 1996a, p. 23). His conception of community is of groups that have no moral purpose, no project and, importantly, refer to nothing but the relations of sociability that constitute it. In this sense, then, postmodern community has no foundation. It exists in temporary groupings, in the flux of life. With this insight, Maffesoli's version of postmodernism differs from that of his main rival Jean Baudrillard, for whom the social has been absorbed by the artificial culture of simulation. For Maffesoli, on the contrary, there are new forms of sociality in certain experiences of community.

We will conclude the survey of postmodern theory of community with this point. We summarize the main points as follows. Postmodern community is neither traditional nor modern; it is sustained by its own reflexivity, creativity and awareness of its limits. Postmodern conceptions of community stress the fluidity of relations between self and other, leading to a view of community as open rather than closed. The upshot of all of this is a transformative notion of community which fills the place of mass culture. Postmodern communities emerge to fill the vacuum in contemporary society that has come with the opening up of culture to expressivist kinds of individualism. While these ideas can be criticized on the grounds that the kind of community they give expression to is highly indeterminate and indefinite (Burns, 2001), the suspension of the moment of closure offers an important corrective to the traditional conceptions of community as static and ordered.

LIMINAL COMMUNITIES: EVERYDAY LIFE, FRIENDSHIP, NEW AGE TRAVELLERS

The argument so far is that the postmodern community is to be understood as a community beyond unity and identity. Rejecting both society and tradition, postmodern community is a new kind of grouping. Everyday life offers many examples of small groups which can be seen as embodying community. What is characteristic of these is their temporary and liminal nature. Their liminality consists of their location in those 'in-between' spaces which are beginning to have growing importance in people's lives.[5] The airport lounge, the commuting train, the leisure centre, a Starbucks café or the shopping centre are examples of liminal – albeit it slackened 'anti-structural' – places in late modern life, for in these 'in-transit' sites people are suspended between other activities but in a way that has a certain reality of its own.

The forms of sociation to be found in these places are hardly constitutive of community in any traditional sense, but there is a sense in which they do take a communal form. Some critics see these non-organic spaces simply as 'non-places' and therefore alien to social life. This is the view of Marc Augé in his book *Non-Places*, when he describes non-places as purely for 'solitary contractuality' as opposed to the organically social of lived places (Augé, 1995, p. 94). However, an alternative view may see these spaces as a domesticated liminality and constitutive of a certain kind of sociation based on temporary groupings. This can be on many levels. Rather than being symbolically constituted, the liminal community is often sustained by non-verbal sociation, as in the grouping of commuters who travel every day between work and home. They may not recognize each other personally and may be on quite different trajectories, but the reality of the liminal situation creates a certain community that is abstract but having its own self-consciousness. In this example the liminal community also has, and is often sustained by a reflexive moment, for only when something unusual happens will there be any verbal interaction. Only in the extreme case will such a community have any more reality than a consciousness of communality. An example of what Giorgio Agamben has called 'the community to come' that is part of all experiences of community might be a rail disaster. In Britain in October 2000 a rail crash occurred at Hatfield junction in Greater London in which four passengers were killed and many injured. This occurred in the wake of a series of major rail crashes in Britain in the late 1990s.[6] Survivors spoke of their emotions and feelings for their fellow-travellers in a way that was unusual. In the context too of press and media giving more attention to personal experience and life-stories, an ethic of what had been liminal community was constructed out of the shared experience of trauma and grief. This was also the case in New York after the terror attacks on 11 September 2001. United in grief, anger and in incomprehension, New York witnessed an unusual degree of community spirit that was sustained by the experience of death. These examples of public grief are indicative of what Blanchot has described as the close link between community and death.

In this context of everyday life there is also the question of communities of taste, a theme discussed by Scott Lash (1994) in his attempt to find an alternative to the individualism that underlies the approaches of Beck and Giddens on reflexivity. Although having a more durable form than liminal community, contemporary fashion may be said to constitute forms of sociation in which the 'I' and the 'We' are neutralized in a way that does not obliterate the autonomy of the self. This was the central idea of the sociology of Georg Simmel and has a contemporary resonance in taste cultures and lifestyles today. These are 'elective communities' in Maffesoli's sense, in that one decides to be part of them, and they are non-binding in that they are not based on strong symbolic bonds but on very temporary associations. The shared nature of lifestyles based on taste can be purely visual and with little normative content. With regard to their liminality, this consists in the transgressively coded nature of much of fashion, where a coded subversion of the status quo may be found. However, there is little doubt that such taste communities can offer only a very limited kind of community. As Jukka Gronow (1997, p. 171) has argued, they are in a constant state of being born and dying out, and as a result it may be better not to term such forms of sociation communities.

Another example of postmodern community which avoids some of these difficulties is friendship, where belonging has a less symbolic form. Although not explicitly advocating a theory of postmodern community, the sociologist Ray Pahl has offered an interesting account of new dynamics of group connections in an insightful study of friendship (Pahl, 2001). His argument is that friendship is becoming increasingly important in social relations and replacing family and kin relations. Friends are taking over various tasks, duties and functions from the traditional family and community. The traditional communities, where the family was central, are often merely nostalgic, with little basis in real social relations. Pahl claims personal networks based on friends are playing a crucial role today, and may even be sustaining the family in terms of providing support. Since people are more likely not to be living close to their own parents they must rely on other kinds of support in dealing with the practical aspects relating to child care, illness and the crises of everyday life. For these problems proximity is important and with the growing incorporation of women into the labour force, rising divorce and separation, new social bonds are needed to cope with increased stress, insecurity, work and emotional pressures. The two- or single-parent family is not always a self-sufficient unit and underlying it is very often a personal community of friends, which may well include members of the wider family who will frequently have much the same function and status as other friends. The reconsitution of the family today may be seen in much the same way as the transformation of community. The family is not disappearing, but simply taking a different form (Beck and Beck-Gernsheim, 2002, pp. 85–100). Both the family and community are becoming more and more pluralized and individuated.

The atomization of society by consumption and work is unlikely to sustain social integration. Thus it might be the case that personal identities and group ties may be shaped increasingly by informal networks outside work and the family. Given the growing importance of networks more generally in contemporary society, it is not at all implausible that friendship may be playing a similar role. Friendship may thus be seen as a flexible and de-territorial kind of community that can be mobilized easily depending on circumstances, and can exist on 'thick' as well as 'thin' levels, for friendship comes in many forms. Cutting across the private and the public spheres and with its emphasis on choice, it also has the features of postmodern community. Friendship has mostly been seen as a purely personal relationship between two people[7] but it is also, as Pahl demonstrates, constitutive of a social bond and one that can give rise to 'personal communities' appropriate for the twenty-first century. In these personal communities, identity and social usefulness are combined in a high degree of functionality.

Finally, we consider the case of New Age travellers. Unlike the other kinds of community discussed in this chapter this concerns a more explicit liminality. New Age travellers are the quintessential postmodern liminal communities. They are not subcultures which subvert the dominant culture, but are literally travellers who transgress into the margins of society. Modernity has always been interested in those ambivalent 'places on the margin' – dangerous, far-off places, the clandestine, the carnivalesque – which were symbolically excluded but at the same time exerted a certain fascination (Shields, 1991). Modern tourism and religious pilgrimages have incorporated such liminal spaces into the organization of space and defused it of its otherness. Such spaces, which were always socially constructed, have been re-created by New Age travellers, whose collective identity is shaped in transgression. As Hetherington has argued in his study of New Age travellers, they help to establish and maintain boundaries through the act of transgression (Hetherington, 2000, pp. 20–1).

New Age travellers appeared in Britain in the late 1970s and consist of new mobile communities drawn from quite diverse class backgrounds. They share a rejection of the dominant values of work, respectability and family, seeking alternative lifestyles based on a sustainable and more organic way of life. They may be seen as expressions of post-material values, and represent a purely 'cultural' social movement. Rather than wanting to change the dominant society, New Age travellers retreat from it in search of a romantic alternative in which freedom is dominant. But freedom can be found only in liminal moments or in the extended space of the road and where the point is the suspension of arrival. Unlike urban sub-cultural movements, these nomadic communities are to be found in marginal places in the British countryside, especially places associated with Celtic or mystical traditions, such as Stonehenge. As Hetherington points out, this results in the curious paradox that in rejecting the dominant values of society, they are also living in the spaces constructed by that culture, such as a certain – and mostly imaginary – notion of the English countryside and its cultural and historical heritage. It is more this loss of parts of an English identity that travellers identify with rather than with a dominant sense of what it is to be English (Hetherington, 2000, p. 117).

Differing from other travellers, such as gypsies and tinkers, in their counter-cultural and middle-class origins, New Age travellers have created a community based on life on the road. This is a postmodern community because of the emphasis on self-identity (Heelas, 1996). Like other groups in society, these travellers also seek self-identity. The need to transgress into liminal spaces is what sustains New Age travellers in their quest for identity. Thus they typically travel to festivals where a carnivalesque spirit sustains the liminal space of the travellers' existence. Carnivals and festivals have been important in defining transgression and its limits in western culture (Stallybrass and White, 1986). In doing so, they have defined the normal community, but they have also given rise to alternative communities which have created forms of belonging around the liminal space of the group. They thus identify positively with marginality and with symbolic exclusion.

In his study of New Age travellers, Hetherington sees a connection with the romantic cult in modernity and makes a comparison with the German youth culture in the period prior to the First World War. The rejection of the dominant values of society as spiritless for a romantic and charismatic cult of friendship, wandering and a return to myth suggests some parallels. While there is undoubtedly a romantic trend in modern culture, New Age travellers have a different kind of community, which is more individuated and democratic. Unlike the German youth movement, there is no comparable political aspiration or organization form and the break with the dominant culture is stronger.

The New Age movement more generally may be seen as an expression of postmodern community. According to Paul Heelas the New Age movement exemplifies the detraditionalization of the self and an expressivist kind of community that extends beyond tradition (Heelas, 1996). But as Heelas indicates, the New Age movement has become institutionalized and much more mainstream today, losing its connection with liminality, anti-structure and the counter-culture. This suggests a certain failure of the kind of community that it gave rise to, which, in the terms of Victor Turner, requires anti-structure to sustain it. It is no longer possible to separate structure and anti-structure in the way it may have made sense for Victor Turner.

To draw this discussion to a close, it is observed that there are several important expressions of postmodern community. The previous part of the chapter looked at some abstract philosophical discussions which all point to a conception of community beyond unity and based on less rigid forms of belonging than what would have been characteristic of more traditional forms of community. Relating some of these ideas to sociological studies, some approximations have been found in forms of urban experience in contemporary society where abstract community is found. Characterizing this as one that occurs in liminal space, further examples were found in groupings as diverse as friendship networks and New Age travellers.

CONCLUSION

The forms of postmodern community considered in this chapter are based on the notion of the openness of community. Many of these philosophical ideas may be related to examples of community emerging in liminal space. This is less evident in the case of friendship-based, personal communities, for these have become significant forms of social organization today. However, even in these cases group boundaries are also ambivalent and not based on an underlying unity, as may have been the case with modernist community. These examples of postmodern community tend to refer to weak forms of community, albeit ones that are significant for much of urban experience where thick and thin are becoming increasingly blurred. The reality is that most communal relationships are composed of both of these forms. Nowhere is this more clear than in the case of cosmopolitan communities.

8

COSMOPOLITAN COMMUNITY
Between the local and the global

The current situation of community has been greatly transformed by globalization. While globalization has fragmented many forms of local community, it has led to the reinvention of others. Some of the most pervasive expressions of community today are transnational. As we saw in Chapter 4, Manuel Castells has argued that many urban social movements have been greatly empowered by globalization, one dimension of which is 'glocalization' – the mixing of the local and the global.[1] 'We are not living in a global village, but in customized cottages globally produced and locally distributed' (Castells, 1996, p. 341). Globalization does not operate 'top-down', but can also provide new political, economic and cultural opportunities for locally based groups to reinvent themselves. The local–global nexus is particularly interesting with regard to new expressions of community.

The main contention of this chapter is that new kinds of community – which might be called cosmopolitan community

– are produced in the mixing of the local and global, the chief characteristic of which is a form of community that is not limited by space or by time. Community has become deterritorialized and scattered in many forms and places. But what is distinctive about these new expressions of 'community beyond propinquity'[2] is that they are also interlinked by communicative and transnational processes. Cosmopolitan communities could thus be said to be communicative communities and to represent the most post-traditional of all kinds of community.

In Chapter 1 I argued that the cosmopolitan face of the community was present in earlier expressions of community, such as in Christianity and in many of the political ideologies of the modern age. But, as we saw in Chapter 2, community became seen more and more as culturally constructed, and in other chapters we looked at political community and local community. The question of global, or cosmopolitan, community will now be discussed. We identify two main kinds of cosmopolitan community, namely world community and transnational community. World communities are those that aspire to be global in reach and recognize only one world and universal humanity. Transnational communities on the other hand have their roots in the local and see the global world as a means of achieving their aspirations. They often take a hybrid form, although many are not hybrid. World and transnational communities are frequently in battle with each other, for in many cases transnational community may be a reaction to world communities. In Chapter 9 we look at virtual communities which are more evenly balanced between the local and global poles and are sustained almost entirely by communication. Globalization offers all these forms of community with powerful opportunities for expression.

It is likely that these forms of cosmopolitanism will become highly significant types of community in the twenty-first century. In speaking of cosmopolitan community as opposed to cultural, political or local community, it is not being claimed that cosmopolitan community is fundamentally different. Rather the claim being made is that cosmopolitan community represents a new level of community, allowing cultural, political and local themes to resonate in a new key and unhindered by the constraints of space and time. No longer constrained by the frontiers of the national state, cosmopolitan community has become a powerful force in the world today (see Thompson, 1998).

The following analysis commences with a few theoretical remarks on community beyond society. This is followed by an account of world community and transnational community.

COMMUNITY BEYOND SOCIETY

Classical sociology was preoccupied with the problem of the survival of community in modern society. Society was in tension with community. Today a new debate has arisen which can be related to globalization, which is fulfilling the role that modernization and rationalization had for classical sociology. This concerns the possibility that society itself may be in demise as a result of the global age. It is interesting to see that the debate is not too different from the community versus society debate in classical sociology and suffers from all the defects of that debate.

An assumption current in much of contemporary sociological theory is that 'society' is a creation of modernity; more specially it is an expression of the geopolitical contours of the nation-state. By equating society with a territorial entity, for example, the nation-state, theorists such as John Urry (2000) not too surprisingly come to the conclusion that society is now obsolete and sociology needs to replace it with new categories. For Urry, the alternative to society is mobilities and to which new kinds of community are possible.[3] Community is thus seen as more amenable to mobility than is society and has a resonance in the global society in which we live. This argument is interesting for many reasons, not least in rehabilitating community as a category appropriate to the global age. However, two qualifications must be made to this thesis.

First, society is not being replaced by something else. It makes little sense defining community in relational terms and as a flexible and mobile category if society is to be attributed all the characteristics that were once given to community. Neither community nor society are territorial categories. They refer to different kinds of social relations and, as I have argued throughout this book, they are overlapping. Societies today are becoming more and more interpenetrating and as a result the forms of belonging in them can take a variety of forms, from transnational to local.

Second, globalization is not bringing about the end of the nation-state but its reconstitution. States are not disappearing and nor are nations. To be sure, states are less able to secure authoritative definitions of the nation and do not control all the forces at work within and beyond them, but they are still powerful actors. There is also much to indicate that today globalization has been arrested. It is possible to speak of a slowing down of globalization, which is being checked by the resurgent state, nationalism and indeed also community. From the 'slow food' movement in Europe to anti-globalization movements to resurgent nationalism and religious movements, the national community has become a powerful force in the world.

One point is clear about the kind of community that has emerged today with globalization: it has lost any connection with the late nineteenth-century German notion of *Gemeinschaft*. This concept has become discredited both politically and intellectually. Politically, in Europe it has been too much associated with populist politics and regressive romanticist ideas, for instance, the Heideggerian appeal to the *Volk* of the soil and blood or Tönnies' naive belief in the recovery of a pastoral age. Intellectually, it has been discredited by what Craig Calhoun has called a secularization of the concept of community from a morally valued way of life to a sociological variable (Calhoun, 1980). Politically, in Europe, the German notion of *Gemeinschaft* was overshadowed by the French term *communauté* and the English word 'community' in the period following the Second World War. Bo Stråth has pointed out that the concept of community in the Paris Treaty of 1951 and the Rome Treaty of 1957, which led to the formation of the European Union, designated an aspiration to a unity that did not exist.[4] One might say it referred to a unity to come. The French and English term *community* reflected a more positive idea than the German *Gemeinschaft*. However, the German term itself gradually lost its *Volk*ish resonances in the growing international climate of the 1960s.

WORLD COMMUNITY

World community is the opposite to local community and is largely the negation of community, as traditionally understood face-to-face encounters in a shared habitus and territory. Insofar as community is based on symbolic differences between relatively homogeneous groups, it cannot be anything on a wider scale since there must be a clearly defined community of reference. However, as we have seen, this is not the only face of community and there have been many expressions of world community. It has already been remarked in Chapter 1 that Christianity, Islam and communism were based on the quest for world community. Even though nationally specific traditions emerged, these were among the most influential forms of world community in history. Many secret organizations such as the Freemasons were globally organized and based on a world consciousness. The struggle for human rights had always been based on the essential unity of humankind. The new social movements, discussed in Chapter 6, were of course also based on a notion of world community. The ecological ethic of global responsibility was very important in giving substance to much empty rhetoric. Democracy itself has been one of the most global of all movements in the modern age. The aspiration for democracy has been one of the most remarkable expressions of a global consciousness and the legitimation of world community as a goal and ideal.

The idea of world community was given a major impetus by the British government in 2001, in the wake of the bombing in New York on 11 September. There is some justification for the view that global terrorism may become the defining event in late modernity. The British Prime Minister Tony Blair appealed to world community as a justification for military action against the alleged perpetrators and their sponsors (although in this postmodern war it is difficult to tell the difference). The terrorist attack was widely believed to have been an attack not on America but on the 'world community' and thus deserved a response from the world. Although this interpretation has been hotly debated, given the overwhelming symbolic significance of the World Trade Center as the centre of American capitalism and the simultaneous attack on the Pentagon, it was the main justification for the support given by the British government for the American-led counter-offensive against Afghanistan. In a major speech on 2 October 2001 at the British Labour Party's annual conference, Tony Blair used the word 'community' seventeen times.[5]

'There is a coming together. The power of community is asserting itself', he announced. Answering the rhetorical question of 'how can the world be a community', he argued that globalization has led to a situation in which the interests of all countries are becoming more and more inextricably linked in many crucial areas. Tying the assertion of world community to 'a capacity for compassion as for force', the issue, he argued, 'is how to use the power of community to combine it with justice'. The speech went on to appeal to 'the power of community' in national politics – 'The governing idea of modern social democracy is community' – and in international politics: 'This is a moment to seize. The kaleidoscope has been shaken. The pieces are in flux.

Soon they will settle again. Before they do, let us reorder the world around us. Today, humankind has the science and technology to destroy itself or to provide prosperity to all. Yet science can't make that choice for us. Only the moral power of a world acting as a community can.' The speech concludes: 'By the strength of our common endeavour we achieve more together than we can living alone. For those people who lost their lives on 11 September and those that mourn them; now is the time for the strength to build that community. Let that be their memorial.'

This is one of the clearest – if somewhat banal – statements of world community. For Tony Blair world community is based on a moral view of the world. Whether in the sphere of national or international politics, community is an essential resource. As discussed in Chapter 4, the political programme of Britain's New Labour under Tony Blair had been highly communitarian in its self-understanding. The appeal to community suited the agenda of third-way politics. Anyone familiar with this movement's political and intellectual agenda will know that third-way politics extends beyond the national context to embrace global politics and markets.[6] The appeal to community suggests something that extends both beyond the national state and within it to something deeper and more personal than the *Gesellschaft* of society. Community – the *Gemeinschaft* of society – avoids the particularity of nationalism and can lend itself easily to globality. The 11 September terrorist attack opened a space for politics to be redefined around world community. In contrast to the 'new world order' announced by the former US President George Bush in 1991 during the Gulf War, 'the power of community' that Tony Blair invoked justified itself less in the interests of national security than in justice and community. But it has an undeniable military objective and reflects the need for the state to find a new role for its military apparatus. In the post-military era of relative peace in the western world – the likelihood of a war between the western states is remote – the state must redefine military power. Consequently new kinds of security are now required which go far beyond the traditional concerns of the interstate system and central to which is the need to be able to deal with international terrorism and internationally organized crime. Issues of national security will have to be discussed increasingly in the context of international co-operation.

While Tony Blair's speech appealing to the power of community to refine the world, reflects a view of world community as one shaped by national governments, others have looked for world community more in the context of global civil society. This shifts the emphasis from the state as the main actor to a variety of non-state and state actors. Conceptions of this cosmopolitan democracy vary from David Held's scenario of a world government based on a revised model of the United Nations to visions of postnational governance based on more informal fora and in which inter-national non-governmental organizations would play a more prominent role (Boli and Thomas, 1997, 1999; Falk, 1995; Held, 1995). For some a world community comes only in the form of a postnational world in which the state will be a very reduced entity, having been displaced by a network of democratic bodies and agents. Whether world community will be manifest in a global constitution and guaranteed by the international community of states or is secured by a wider variety of actors and discourses is one of the main dividing lines in the current literature on cosmopolitanism.[7] It seems reasonable to suggest that world community in this sense of global civil society is made up of four actors: states, non-state actors (such as non-governmental organizations), international governmental agencies (such as the UN, the International Red Cross, the EU and other transnational organizations), and finally international law. These are the institutional forms in which world community is manifest.

In addition to these, it is also important to add that an even more important expression of world community is in the formation of cultural discourses. The power of community consists in the emergence of definitions, principles and cognitive models for imagining the world. In essence, the power of community is the power of communication. The ecological movement, human rights movements, humanitarian organizations and a whole range of other social movements have brought about a major transformation in perceptions of the world. New discourses have emerged around, for instance, a global ethic of responsibility for nature and for the alleviation of suffering (Strydom, 2002). These ways of thinking will ultimately be more significant in shaping world community than the actions of states. This non-statist sense of world community points to common discourses, which arise in many different contexts – in local and national contexts as much as in the international arena – rather than to something like a 'new world order'. Viewing world community in this way, as something discursively constructed in communicative flows, avoids reductionism. As has been argued in this book, community is not something already formed and expressed in certain observable effects, such as symbolic structures. Nor is it reducible to specific social agents or institutions. It exists in the medium of its expression. World community, as in the example of Tony Blair's speech above, is constructed in a discourse and does not correspond directly to an underlying reality. For this reason world community is elusive; it can be claimed by many social actors, from government leaders to movement activists.

There is a point at which world community fades into what might be called transnational community. Some of the major discourses of world community, as in the speech by Tony Blair, assert one world, but world community can also be less specific in its designation of who the subject of political action is. Once the subject becomes unspecified, more and more actors can enter into it, subverting the discourse and adapting it to new ends. In this situation the discourse of world community fragments into many projects. It is in this context that we may consider transnational community.

TRANSNATIONAL COMMUNITY

Transnational community arises in the appropriation of the global by the local. It differs from world community in its association with local forms of attachment. In the sense used here, transnational communities operate in the global context but are the projects of locally based communities. While one of the major expressions of world community is the global civil society – and the growing international public sphere – transnational communities owe their existence to migration, the massive movement of peoples across the globe and, unlike the global civil society, do not presuppose a convergence in discourses. Transnational communities are variously migratory, diasporic, hybrid in their composition. Their cosmopolitanism derives from mobility by which they transcend place and the resulting cultural mixing produces identities that are constantly in the process of definition.[8] In our age of migration, nomadic cultures flow into each other and become mixed. This can result in pure hybrid cultures or in ones that are to varying degrees based on an original or dominant ethnic identity. In the case of diasporas, to follow Robin Cohen's typology, there can be victim diasporas, trade diasporas, cultural diasporas, imperial diasporas and labour diasporas (Cohen, 1997).

Interpretations of diasporas vary. British postcolonialists such as Paul Gilroy, Stuart Hall and Homi Bhabha stress the colonial legacy of the black diasporic communities whose consciousness is formed in the context of a double consciousness in which the legacy of the past and the resistance of the present shape the collective identity of the diaspora. In contrast to the bipolar formulation of the black diaspora, Aihwa Ong highlights less the dual and reactive characteristic of global diasporas or marginality, for many of these diasporas were not shaped exclusively by colonialism and are products of a new cultural and economic self-confidence (Ong, 1999). The Chinese diaspora, for instance, she argues, exists in a post-developmental era which is highly favourable to the new class of Chinese professionals from Southeast Asian countries who migrate in multiple directions to several different countries. A transnational Chinese community has emerged which is highly de-territorial and flexible. This Asian diaspora, she claims, is characterized by multiple geographies, and not by a dual consciousness. The result is that Chinese has become an open signifier. But the diaspora can take many forms, as already noted. While postcolonial authors stress the black or Atlantic diaspora and Ong the Chinese one, it should be noted that many diasporas exist in borderlands, not in the metropolitan cores of the west or the booming cities of Southeast Asia. This would suggest moving beyond an emphasis on the diaspora to a wider emphasis on migratory movements, since not all transnational migrations constitute diasporas, and the term itself suggests a religious underpinning of identity. Moreover, the postcolonial approach stresses too much the hybrid nature of transnational communities and the constant production of difference. Although this is more pronounced in postcolonial postmodernist approaches, such as in the work of Spivak, where difference is celebrated for its own sake, the tendency has also become part of the growing literature on diasporas (Spivak, 1987). But not all diasporas, or transnational communities, are quite as hybrid as is often suggested and there is a point at which hybridity itself becomes a new substantive identity. In the case of many transnational communities there is a dominant ethnic or religious identity that places limits on the production of difference.

One of the best examples of transnational communities is the refugee camp which is formed out of local and global relations and where a potent sense of community can emerge from trauma, collective memories and the experience of exile. According to the World Refugee Survey 2000, the total number of internationally displaced persons (IDPs) in the world in 2000 was estimated to be more than 35 million, which exceeds the population in 160 countries and is growing every year. More than 14 million are refugees in their own countries and in ninety-six of the world's some 191 countries, more than half are directly linked to uprooted populations. Millions of IDPs are housed in refugee camps all over the world where exiled communities are formed in these most liminal of places. Liminality more than hybridity is what is distinctive about the refugee camp, most of which are located in borderlands. Diasporic groups constitute communities in contexts as different as multicultural western cities where they eventually settle and the temporary exile of the refugee camp. In the liminal space of the refugee camp locality is produced on two levels. Many refugee camps are relatively uniform, containing one national or ethnic group that has fled, generally from a neighbouring country from where it has sought refuge, as in the case of Afghans fleeing into Pakistan from the Taliban regime or Palestinians who fled to Lebanon following the Israeli occupation. Whether under the protection of the host country's government or an international relief agency, the refugee camp will often reproduce the spatial geography of the original villages from which the refugees were forced to flee. In the refugee camp intense identities of belonging emerge out of shared experiences arising from the past as well as the present circumstances of discrimination and marginalization. In the refugee camp, place is crucial, since the refugee camp is first and foremost a spatially organized area where space is highly bounded and controlled.

According to the anthropologist Julie Peteet, over nearly a fifty-year period of exile, Palestinian refugees in camps in Lebanon have developed a sense of community, with shared experiences arising from displacement and political expectations arising from this experience of exile (Peteet, 2000, pp. 200–3).[9] In the refugee camp, cultural, political, local and cosmopolitan community combine to produce a powerful sense of community as one of collective empowerment and action. The community that took shape in the refugee camps was strengthened by the reproduction of the pre-1948 villages, with many quarters in the camps named after the original villages. These village boundaries gradually became associated with the political organization of the resistance movement. But community can also be located on the level of the camp itself, and not just with the level of locality. Each camp in Lebanon has its own community identity based on its contribution to the resistance movement.

> In exile, the resistance movement fostered a sense of commu-
> nity, and these sentiments were then given organizational
> expression in the political, social, and military activities and
> institutions of the movement. The resistance also linked
> regional groups into units that were cohesive and able to act in
> unison, particularly militarily.
>
> (Peteet, 2000, p. 201)

The case of the refugee camp represents a striking contrast to the other example of the transnational community mentioned above: the diasporic community in the west where it has partly settled and in many cases has achieved a high degree of integration and even of differentiation. In the latter case the transnational community is situated neither in home nor in exile, but in both. Transnational communities have brought about major cultural change both in their countries of exile and in their original homeland. In the countries of the European Union, immigrants have acquired important rights and have been significant in forging the recognition of their status. The result is that national citizenship has been displaced by postnational membership of the polity, with citizenship rights no longer confined exclusively to nationals (Kastoryano, 2002; Soysal, 1994). In many cases the original homeland is a very distant memory, especially for the second and third generation who may no longer speak the primary language of the ethnic community.

But memory is something constructed, and the homeland can become more real in the construction of imagined communities of memory by nostalgic third generation immigrants who no longer seek the integration their parents or grandparents sought. The result can be a certain de-differentiation, as in the rise of new communal identities based on resistance to globalization and resistance to earlier waves of modernization.

In the new politics of difference, the transnational community can produce new streams of consciousness that awaken an aspiration for the cause of the diaspora. These communities of memory can be very powerful since they transcend any concrete experiences but are produced in the collective consciousness of a transnational community, which in reality may be as differentiated as any other globally scattered group but in terms of its identity will be highly homogeneous. In these memories the collective subject is constituted anew as an imaginary presence. The memory of trauma, arising from marginality, discrimination and forced exile, can be a potent element in these communal identities. Manuel Castells has made the argument that under such pressures, ethnicity is overshadowed by other cultural and political forces, which reappropriate it: 'Ethnicity, while being a fundamental feature of our societies, especially as a source of discrimination and stigma, may not induce communes on its own. Rather, it is likely to be processed by religion, nation, and locality, whose specificity it tends to reinforce' (Castells, 1997, p. 65). His argument is that many social actors are turning away from or resisting the individualization of identity that the modern world has brought and are instead seeking a new and enchanted identity in cultural community. They are largely culturally shaped defensive identities that are reactions to the modern world, but they are of course products of modernity and not expressions of dormant historical identities that somehow mysteriously rise at times of crisis. It is suggested, then, that cultural community as expressed in certain kinds of transnationalism may be a retreat from modernity and a reaction to its threatening forms of individualization and differentiation. Ethnicity needs more globally organized discourses to produce something like a transnational community. Ethnicity is based on primary bonds, Castells argues, which lose their significance when transposed to a more global level of cultural reproduction.

Distinguishing between legitimizing identities, which are based on the dominant institutions, resistance identities, which resist domination and generally derive from marginalized groups, and project identities, which aim at building new institutions, Castells argues that community is largely reactive to globalization against which it offers a defensive 'communal heaven'. Resistance identities can become project identities, as in the case of feminism, once they move out of the trenches of resistance to build a new and positive identity. However, resistance identities lead predominantly to the formation of 'communes' or communities, according to Castells:

In contrast to pluralistic, differentiated civil societies, cultural communes display little internal differentiation. Indeed, their strength, and their ability to provide refuge, solace, certainty, and protect, comes precisely from their communal character, from their collective responsibility, canceling individual projects. Thus, in the first stage of reaction, the (re)construction of meaning by defensive identities breaks away from the institutions of society, and promises to rebuild from the bottom up, while retrenching themselves in a communal heaven.

(Castells, 1997, p. 67)

In this view, the contemporary world is full of examples of community as an identity of resistance, ranging from nationalism to religious fundamentalism. The age of globalization is also the age of community. The search for community is a reaction against the globalization in the first instance: that is, a reaction against the breakup of stable social institutions and the continuity of the life-world. It is also a reaction against the progressive currents of the age, such as individualization and the crisis of the patriarchal family. Legitimizing identities seem unable to maintain their function, and the result, in Castells' theory, is a battle between resistance identities and project identities. His question might be formulated as whether resistance identities might be transformed into project identities. Like Alain Touraine, who believes the struggle between a neocommunitarian identity and instrumental reason is dividing the world, the chances are relatively good for a project identity to emerge (Touraine, 1995, 2000).

While Castells and Touraine are relatively optimistic on this, not all commentators are of the view that something like a new 'subject' – to use Touraine's term – will emerge to reconcile the existing polarities. The new American orthodoxy is that the world is locked in combat between irreconcilable civilizational cultures. Since the Gulf War, but greatly amplified since the terrorist attack on the USA on 11 September 2001, the alleged 'clash of civilizations' has become one of the most discussed 'explanations' of the contemporary situation. Not all accounts of the clash of civilizations are quite as crude as Samuel Huntington's view that the western Christian-democratic culture is faced with a revanchist Islamic-Confucian civilization. Benjamin Barber in *Jihad vs. McWorld* presents a more subtle analysis of global community, which is closer to the positions of Castells and Touraine (Barber, 1996). Against the simple view that there is a one-world order emerging, as argued by Fukuyama (1992), or that there are two religious civilizations locked in an irreconcilable struggle, he describes the global conflict as one between a global culture, based on the values of capitalism, and on the other side a fundamentalist retreat into authoritarian community and tribalist sentiments. His solution is to look to the inclusive values of civil society for an alternative to McWorld and Jihad. 'A global democracy capable of countering the antidemocratic tendencies of Jihad and McWorld cannot be borrowed from some particular nation's warehouse or copied from an abstract constitutional template. Citizenship, whether global or local, comes first' (Barber, 1996, p. 279).

In sum, transnational communities may be said to be major examples of cosmopolitan community. Rejecting the vision of a one-world community and seeking the utopia of locality, transnational communities find in the global order many possibilities to reproduce themselves. In this sense they share with many post-traditional kinds of community a basic communicative form. The communicative possibilities that globalization offers have allowed many traditional forms of community to be reinvented and sustained under the new circumstances that the diaspora encounters.

CONCLUSION

Distinguishing between 'thin' and 'thick' forms of community, world community may be described as thin while transnational communities and cyber or virtual communities – to be considered in Chapter 9 – can take thin or thick forms, depending on the strength of local attachments. These are the main expressions of cosmopolitan community, the chief characteristic of which is communication. While mobility is also very central to all kinds of cosmopolitan community, it is not the critical feature of them. In cosmopolitan community, belonging is highly discursive in that it is constructed around discourses that are never fully closed or embodied in fixed reference points. World community is largely a matter of rhetoric or discursive deliberation (speeches, conferences, summits), virtual community exists only within the communicative and information-based structures of cyberspace (websites, chat-rooms), and transnational communities also owe their existence to communicative links as established by networks of actors. It is in this sense that they are communication communities, and the discourse of belonging that gets articulated in them is one that ultimately can never be closed. The result of this is that the 'unhappy consciousness' which Hegel believed characterized the modern condition now lies at the heart of community, for its basic aspiration – the desire to belong – can never be realized.

Cosmopolitan communication communities are based on discourses of belonging that construct the community of reference in a very open-ended way. In the case of world community, this extends the community of reference to humanity as a whole or the global civil society. Such inclusive forms of community inevitably dilute belonging into a thin universalistic identity. It is also inevitable that this universalistic discourse of community will run up against more particularistic and closed expressions of community. Transnational communities reflect global consciousness too, but in a way that empowers the local, opening it up to new dimensions. Thus while being more open discourses of belonging than traditional local communities, transnational communities have a stronger sense of closure than one-world community.

One of the main conclusions to be drawn from the analysis in this chapter, and from the book as a whole, is that community exists in many forms, and that therefore a more differentiated approach to it is required. There is not one kind of community that is more 'real' than other forms, or that all kinds of community are derivative of a basic community. There are multiple forms of community – traditional face-to-face communities, virtual communities, transnational communities, one-world community – which often complement each other. Thus transnational communities can be sustained by virtuality and can enhance as much as emanate from traditional local communities. This is the subject of Chapter 9.

9

VIRTUAL COMMUNITY
Belonging as communication

No discussion of community today can be complete without some consideration of the role technology plays in reshaping social relations. Since Marshall McLuhan's *The Gutenberg Galaxy* in 1962, social thought has entertained the idea of a global community of communication (McLuhan, 1962). To an extent this has now become a reality, but in a different form from what McLuhan imagined. Information and communication technologies have created powerful new expressions of community that go far beyond all hitherto forms of community. In the past, technology was seen as undermining community, but today in the age of 'soft' technologies, community has been given new possibilities for its expression. This necessitates a new approach to community. Some of the most important literature on community is now on the virtual community (Castells, 2001; Jones, 1995; Rheingold, 1993; Shields, 1996; Smith and Kollock, 1999).

Technologically mediated communities – cyber-community or virtual community – are bringing about new kinds of social groups, which are polymorphous, highly personalized and often expressive, but they can also take more traditional forms, reconstituting families and rural areas and even political movements. In these communities, which are often acted out in the global context, belonging has been reshaped radically, leading many to question the very possibility of belonging as it disappears into the flow of communication. The result is that place, locality and symbolic ties are being drained of any content, and in their place are more fluid and temporary forms of social relations sustained only by processes of communication outside of which they have no reality.[1] Whether these communicative moments constitute communities is hard to say and a lot depends on what is meant by the term *community*.

We begin with a look at some of the issues that are at stake in virtual community, in particular the question of the relation of the real to the virtual. In the second section three of the main theorists of virtual community – Rheingold, Castells, Calhoun – are critically assessed. In the final section the major debates on the impact of virtual community are critically discussed. The principal contention of this chapter is that virtual communities are no less real than traditional or other kinds of community and that their distinctive nature consists in their ability to make communication the essential feature of belonging. Communication is the medium in which belonging is today being expressed in its most important ways. This leads to the argument that virtual communities are only one form of community and exist alongside other kinds of community.

TECHNOLOGY AND THE TRANSFORMATION
OF COMMUNITY

The social forms of technology are varied, but three can be identified: the tool model, the utopian model and the cultural model. In the tool model technology is a means to achieve a humanly defined end. The classical understanding of technology was that it was a tool to fashion something. Technology was an instrument in the service of human need or purpose. Modernity added to this a second form of technology: technology as an end in itself. The Enlightenment produced a great faith in the ultimate value of technology which saw it as driven by science and had the aim of mastering nature. With the advancement of modernity, technology became more and more utopian in its aspiration. Today, a third kind of technology has come into existence. The new technologies – communication and information technologies, biotechnologies, new reproductive technologies, surveillance technologies – are driven less by science than by technology and markets, frequently taking the form of techno-science. Their capacity to reconstitute the world is immense, but they are very different from the technologies of high modernity: they are more interwoven into the fabric of everyday life; they have the capacity to change human nature itself; many of them are 'soft' technologies in contrast to the 'hard' technologies of modernity; and they are characterized by speed, reflecting the 'fast capitalism' of the global age.[2]

The new technologies are 'cultural' in the sense that they are more and more embedded in forms of social life rather than being concentrated in, for example, industrial complexes, factories, offices and so on. Technology has become intermeshed with everyday life and with life projects; it has become 'socialized', and as a result we are far beyond the classical and modernist conception of technology as neutral or as an inherent good in itself. Mobile phones, e-mail, the Internet are among the most social forms of technology ever devised, since they have eliminated the distance which all previous communication technologies required. Digital networks are characterized by decentralized access, simultaneity and interconnectivity (Sassen, 2002, p. 366). These are characteristics conducive to communication, especially global communication. It is in this context that we consider the role of information and communication technologies in shaping new kinds of fluid community.

The first and most important thing to note about the emergence of virtual community is that it is a form of community mediated by a highly personalized technology. By technology we do not simply mean an instrument or non-social apparatus, for technology has become socialized today and many moral issues are inseparable from it. We should therefore set aside any notion that technology and community are irreconcilable. The new technologies are as likely to be found in the home as in the factory.

A second point also needs to made. We should abandon the distinction between real and imaginary communities. As Benedict Anderson has shown in his famous book *Imagined Communities*, with the coming of modernity and print mediated discourse, communities had to develop the cognitive capacity to image themselves for the simple reason that the kinds of community that are formed with modernity – the nation, for instance – cannot be sustained by traditional face-to-face means (Anderson, 1983). Information and communication technologies are a development of the print cultures described by Anderson. Mark Poster in *The Second Media Age* develops this imaginary dimension of community with the argument that 'the Internet and virtual reality open the possibility of new kinds of interactivity such that the idea of an opposition of real and unreal community is not adequate to specify the differences between modes of bonding, serving instead to obscure the manner of the historical construction of forms of community' (Poster, 1995, p. 35).

The virtual community is more akin to the postmodern community beyond unity and where a new kind of individualism has emerged around ephemeral realities and de-massified social relations. These might be called 'thin' communities, as Bryan Turner argues, in contrast to the 'thick' or organic communities of tradition (Turner, 2001, p. 29). As thin communities, they are not based on strong ties and are often communities of strangers. The Internet brings together strangers in a sociality often based on anonymity and where a 'new intimacy' is found in which politics and subjectivity are intertwined. 'The contemporary internet could be regarded as a global market of strangers exchanging information and as a consequence creating a thin community. As local cultural identities thicken in response to decolonization, political networks extend through thin channels of exchange' (ibid.). Virtual community is one of the best examples we have of communication communities, since the exclusive aim of the virtual community is the sharing of information in a communicative context outside of which it does not always exist.

Technologically mediated community does not necessarily mean the absence of morality. Kenneth Gergen argues that morality has been reshaped by technology. In order to appreciate this we have to move beyond community as face-to-face relations within a common territory to a sense of community as an open communicative process and which exists in a flexible relation to other kinds of community. In his book the *Saturated Self*, Gergen argues that community as face-to-face relations has been eroded by the technologies of modernity (Gergen, 1991). Modernity has introduced too many distances into everyday life arising from mobilities for face-to-face community to be a reality for most people – home and work are separated, families and friends are scattered, people are going on more and more holidays and so on – who rely increasingly on other forms of communication to sustain their realities, values and agendas (Gergen, 2001, p. 192).

Technologically mediated exchange, whether the telephone, the TV, radio, CD player, Internet, has enhanced the mobilities and also the velocities that people experience in everyday life. Sociologically, there is no reason why these forms of reality are less real than other kinds. This is also stressed by John Urry, for whom mobility is one of the key features of social life today to the point of becoming more significant than the settled forms of living of the past (Urry, 2000). Virtual interactivity is generating new kinds of 'dwellings', he argues. Distinguishing between 'propinquity, localness and communion', he claims that the new electronic places can produce communion without propinquity, because people can imagine themselves as belonging to a virtual community. In this new sphere, where the distinction between travelling and belonging is broken down, locality can be reinvented in the same way as identities can be combined in different ways by digital nomads (Urry, 2000, pp. 73–4).

Virtuality may be said to be a product of modernity which, as Anthony Giddens has put it, 'displaces' the individual and makes place more and more phantasmagoric (Giddens, 1990, p. 140). Modernity is constantly displacing the individual, place, the familiar everyday world and re-embedding these in different contexts, ones in which familiarity and estrangement are recombined. The local shopping mall seems familiar but we know most of the shops are chain stores and thus our sense of community is pervaded by the realization that the global and local are connected. With regard to virtual communities, it is suggested that the opposite is also true: the distant becomes quite close and familiar precisely because of such mechanisms of displacement and re-embedment. In this context, the notion of the 'tyranny of proximity' is relevant.[3]

The information age has brought about a saturation of communication, and with it proximity becomes ever more present in people's lives. The mobile phone, Internet and e-mail have produced not only more, but more intensified, forms of belonging, leading to more not less proximity. But this will be a different kind of promixity from face-to-face proximity.

THEORIES OF VIRTUAL COMMUNITY

As noted above, there is a growing social, scientific and philosophical literature on the possibility of virtual community. However, it is largely underdeveloped and theoretically vague, with assumptions rarely made explicit. Three main theoretical positions may be identified and associated with studies by Howard Rheingold, Manuel Castells and Craig Calhoun, who have all written the most interesting and influential works on virtual community. In this section they will be critically discussed in order to provide a basis for further evaluation of the impact of information and communication technologies.

Howard Rheingold

Howard Rheingold's book *The Virtual Community: Homesteading on the Electronic Frontier* was the first major study of virtual community and a reference point for all subsequent studies. Although, when this was published in 1993, the Internet was far less expansive and information and communication technologies much less developed than they are today, it still remains a classic work on the transformation of belonging.[4] Rheingold viewed the Internet as an alternative reality to existing realities and as having the capacity to transform society. Rather than complement existing relationships, it offered a new and fundamentally different level of interaction. It was on the whole a very positive view of the Internet as an alternative reality to 'real' realities from which people could escape: 'I suspect that one of the explanations for this phenomenon is the hunger for community that grows in the breasts of people around the world as more and more informal public spaces disappear from our real lives' (1993, p. 62). But virtual reality is more than a compensation for the real, it is an escape from the real. A certain assumption of technological determinism lay behind his argument. Information and communication technologies are themselves capable of not only changing social relations but creating new ones. However, what is distinctive about his argument is that virtual communities are 'communities on the Net'. They do not exist in everyday life. The assumption then is that the Internet constitutes communities that otherwise do not exist. This view perhaps reflected the fact that his book was a response to the Internet culture of the mid- to late 1980s in the USA when a relatively small number of users constituted what in effect was a fairly homogeneous community. His argument has been criticized on the grounds that it exaggerates the capacity of the Internet to create new kinds of community and does not see that the forms of community that are sustained by the Internet are not necessarily different from those that exist outside it.[5] Moreover, it is a view that is less applicable to the much more diverse situation that has arisen some two decades later.

In Rheingold's book we have the image of people withdrawing from everyday life to enter the strange world of virtuality where new kinds of relationship and modes of communication are entered into. In a sense, then, this is almost a modernist vision of virtual community; that is a utopia which technology can create and which is a superior kind of community to the concretely existing one. It is a modernist vision in that it sees virtual community as located far from 'real' communities and as quite different. Yet, ironically, this view of community borrows the language of 'real' communities, suggesting that in fact he sees virtual communities as technological versions of traditional communities. The image of place, for instance, is very strong in Rheingold's book, reflecting a view of the Internet as respatializing traditional forms of place such as villages, the home and neighourhoods. Unlike the communicative technologies of modernity such as the post office and telephone, Rheingold thinks the Internet can offer new spaces in which community can be reconstituted in meaningful forms with people with common identities.

Manuel Castells has a different social theory of virtual communities. While sharing much of the confidence of information and communication technologies in Rheingold's theory, Castells locates virtual communities as part of a real virtuality. In short, he avoids the dualism of virtuality and reality that was a feature of Rheingold's book as well as his assumption of thick virtual community. The relation between the virtual and the real is a more complex and reflexive one, with virtuality now a part of the real world – where thick communities are rare.

Manuel Castells

Castells introduced the idea of real virtuality in his major three-volume work, *The Information Age*: 'It is a system in which reality itself (that is, people's material/symbolic) existence is entirely captured, fully immersed in a virtual image setting, in the world of make believe, in which appearances are not just on the screen through which experience is communicated, but they become the experience' (Castells, 1996, p. 373). This level of experience is now seen as a level of reality, not removed from it. Moreover, it has the capacity to transform social relations. Unlike Rheingold, he introduces a differentiated approach to virtual community. There is widespread social and cultural differentiation in terms of the types of users and their purposes. He advanced the hypothesis that 'two very different populations "live" in such virtual communities: a tiny minority of electronic villages "homesteading" in the electronic frontiers, and a transient crowd for whom their casual incursions into various networks is tantamount to exploring several existences under the mode of the ephemeral' (Castells, 1996, p. 362). It is this latter category that is of particular interest to Castells. However, his theory is that, despite differentiation in users, there is a convergence of experience in the new virtual medium, leading to a blurring or de-differentiation in institutional spheres. It is a strong thesis of virtual community becoming itself a new kind of reality that has the capacity to transform social relations.

In a later work, *The Internet Galaxy*, Castells (2001) reassessed the emerging patterns of sociability with the Internet and restated his claim that a virtual community is now a form of social reality. The Internet has been appropriated by social practice, he argues, and to an extent has altered social practice, although Castells is more cautious about claims of this nature and offers a more balanced account. However, he advances a clear thesis that the Internet has a positive effect on social interaction, enhancing democratic possibilities and offering people a more communicative means of ordering their relations. For instance, the use of e-mail, at least by the higher educated, is a means of sustaining networks of friends and family. Castells' theory of the real virtuality of communities of Internet users has shifted to a position which sees this as consisting of changing patterns of sociability and less as a substitute for everyday social relations. With the diminishing significance of geographical proximity as a means of organizing social relations, community becomes shaped by other factors. It is not because people do not live in localities any more – in fact Castells argues that residential mobility may be exaggerated – but because residential locality is not the defining factor in shaping community and therefore cannot be a major factor in the transformation of community. He makes the important observation that in agricultural societies and in early industrialization locality was certainly a factor but this was because it was related to work rather than to the simple fact of residence. Perhaps it is the changing nature of work along with wider social and cultural change that has made the difference, rather than the fact of residential mobility. For Castells the reality of virtual communities consists of their social nature.

New communities are being built out of networks, he argues: 'Networks are built by the choices and strategies of social actors, be it individuals, families, or social groups. Thus, the major transformation of sociability in complex societies took place with the substitution of networks for spatial communities as major forms of sociability' (Castells, 2001). Following Barry Wellman, Castells proposes the term 'personalized communities' to describe these new communities embodied in networks and centred on the individual. Wellman's definition of community is accurate: 'Communities are networks of interpersonal ties that provide sociability, support, information, a sense of belonging, and social identity' (Wellman, 2001, p. 127; quoted in Castells, 2001, p. 127).

This all seems to amount to a conception of virtual community as a 'thin' community. The Internet is effective in maintaining at a distance positive social relations that otherwise would not be sustained, due to the effort involved and perhaps because of the value of the relationship. Virtual communities can support existing relations but rarely create new ones, except those that require the sharing of information. For this reason Castells argues that most on-line communities are 'ephemeral communities', which should be understood as 'networks of sociability'. In this study Castells has reduced the technological determinism of his earlier work. It is not information and communication technology itself that is changing social relations but the emergence of individualism and in particular networked individualism. The significance of virtual communities is that they give form to this kind of individualism. While there are virtual communities that are highly experimental and based on relationships that are entirely virtual, many in fact take the form of supplementing existing relationships. Thus, the best example of the social impact of the Internet may be redefining one of the most traditional of all institutions, namely the family. But what is critical for Castells is that virtual community is in its most important function based on networks of diverse people, allowing them to add a new dimension to their relationship. Thus, families can be sustained as cyber-families; that is, as 'thin' networks of highly personalized individuals who do not otherwise have much in common. It is in this respect that Craig Calhoun disagrees – for him virtual communities have only a limited capacity to unite that which is different.

Craig Calhoun

Craig Calhoun's study of the 'radicalness of tradition' was discussed in Chapter 2 (Calhoun, 1983). Rather than accept the conventional assumption of a break between tradition and modernity, Calhoun argued that there was continuity between the corporatism of the past and modern socialism, with traditional communities providing important structures for shared interests and a capacity for collective action to develop. What is significant, then, is not the binding force of traditional values as such but collective resources and a capacity for collective action. This idea of community as a system of social relationships has been at the centre of a series of papers on the changing nature of community, especially in the context of information and communication technology (Calhoun, 1980, 1986, 1988, 1991, 1992, 1998). Calhoun's theory of community can be contrasted to Castells' in one crucial respect. While Castells modified considerably the 1980s conception of virtual community, as represented for instance by Rheingold and his own earlier arguments about real virtuality, he retained a basic fate in the liberating capacity of the Internet to reconstitute social relations in a new key. In fact he continued to hold to a strong thesis of virtual communities transforming social relations and as major agents of democratization in the networked and global society. Calhoun in contrast offers a more differentiated analysis, which is also more rigorously sociological and cautious in its conclusions.

Calhoun agrees with Castells that indirect or mediated relations are becoming more important. However, he does not locate these entirely as products of the information age or as products of globalization. Large-scale markets, transportation systems, administrative organizations, the nation-state, that all came with the process of modernization, produced such forms of indirect social relationships. While premodern societies depended primarily on direct interpersonal relations, 'modernity is distinguished by the increasing frequency, scale, and importance of indirect social relationship' (Calhoun, 1992, p. 211). This is the social context in which to view virtual communities, which do not mark a break with this trend. Calhoun's argument is that virtual communities must be seen as giving expression to indirect forms of social relationship. We should not exaggerate these forms of relationship and it is important not to misunderstand the differences between direct and indirect interaction: 'the internet matters much more as a supplement to face-to-face community organization and movement activity than as a substitute for it' (Calhoun, 1998, p. 382). In this respect he agrees with Castells. The impact of the Internet is most evident when it reinforces already existing social relations, but – and in this respect he disagrees – the Internet does not necessarily create or promote networks. Most e-mail, for instance, is not with strangers but with family, friends, colleagues or those who share a common life-world. With the expansion in the Internet, thus goes a re-traditionalizing of its impact in the sense that it facilitates and strengthens existing social relations based on common ties, giving them new possibilities for expression and allowing them to adapt to distance. Community is to be understood as a system of social relations, rather than something defined by place. But community also entails belonging in the sense of sharing something:

> Community life can be understood as the life people live in dense, multiplex, relatively autonomous networks of social relationship.

Community life, thus, is not a place or simply a small-scale population aggregate, but a mode of relating, variable in extent. Though communities may be larger than the immediate personal networks of individuals, they can in principle be understood by an extension of the same lifeworld terms.

(Calhoun, 1988, p. 391; see also Calhoun, 1980, 1986)

His thesis differs from Castells' in that he sees the Internet as producing communities of similarities more than strengthening local networks of diverse people. Computer-mediated communication, he argues, adds to existing forms of communication, many of which are already highly mediated and networked, a greater capacity for interaction based on personal choices of taste and culture, what he calls 'categorical identities'. These are then more likely to be communities based on the sharing of a single concern rather than networks that bind people together across many areas of activity. This argument, which is essentially one of making more modest claims for the Internet, differs also from Castells in highlighting some of the negative aspects. The 'compartmentalization of community life is antithetical to the social constitution of a vital public sphere', he says (Calhoun, 1998, p. 389). As an agent of democratization it has lagged far behind its commercial and entertainment possibilities, but this may be more than a lagging behind, since it may be the nature of the Internet to make politics fluid and thus ineffective.

The crux of the problem for Calhoun is that virtual communities once they extend beyond a culturally specific group are thin communities and have only a weak capacity to enhance democratization. Virtual communities certainly exist as communities based on shared identities and whose members may rarely meet. These kinds of community will be ineffective in fostering democracy. His argument thus differs from Castells' in that virtual community does not necessarily create new social and political realities; they strengthen already existing ones, especially in offering a means of linking people with similar taste. But not much that is new is produced. The chances of a more networked society emerging as in Castells' theory must be viewed with caution. When it comes to linking people who are different it is a separate matter, and it is here that there are very major problems with creating democratic possibilities.

In conclusion, of the three approaches looked at above, Calhoun's seems to be the most credible. His argument that community must be theorized in terms of social relationships of belonging is important in grounding the concept of virtual community. The claim that virtual community is a supplement to existing forms of community, which are themselves already despatialized, has been supported by recent sociological research: '"On-line communities" come in very different shapes and sizes, ranging from virtual communities that connect geographically distant people with no prior acquaintance who share similar interests, to settings that facilitate interactions that focus on issues relevant to a geographically defined neighbourhood' (DiMaggio *et al.*, 2001, p. 317). The general conclusion is towards a scaling down of the idea of virtual community to a more differentiated view of the impact of information and communication technologies as offering possibilities for the expression of a wide variety of forms of social belonging rather than the creation of something entirely new.

THE POLITICAL IMPACT OF VIRTUAL COMMUNITY: GAINS AND LOSSES

Despite the conclusion reached so far on the social nature of virtual community we cannot say that virtual communities are unimportant or that information and communication technologies have had little impact on society. We now consider more specifically the political consequences of these technologies as far as political community is concerned. On the one side, there are those who take a largely affirmative view of such developments, while others see it in more critical terms. The affirmative stance is threefold.

First, virtual community empowers people. Manuel Castells, as we have seen above, has greatly stressed the opportunities for empowerment in the new communication and information technologies. In particular, people who are more likely to be excluded from other kinds of power, such as women, the disabled and young people, can be empowered by communication and information technologies. There is thus a communitarian – in the sense of civic republican – strand to these arguments of social inclusion being fostered by information and communication technologies.

Second, virtual community is held to be more democratic than other forms of communication. What is typically emphasized in this context is the interactive nature of the virtual community in comparison to other forms of communication, such as TV, which involve passivity. The virtual community is also allegedly horizontally organized, as opposed to being hierarchical. This argument is related to assumptions about the nature of globalization and has been advocated by both Giddens (1998) and Castells (1996). However, in Giddens' 'third-way' theory this is especially pronounced. This is a view of globalization as enabling rather than restricting democracy.

Third, a postmodern inspired argument is that virtual communities are more experimental and innovative with respect to new identities and can create new kinds of experience which traditional communities cannot achieve. In this case what is stressed is less community consisting of ties and obligations than community in terms of constructing identities. Much of the positive literature on virtual community has been influenced by postmodern ideas of cultural mixing and hybridity.

The arguments that information and communication technologies constitute a new kind of political community have not gone unchallenged. The critical positions may be summarized as follows.

First, there is the liberal inspired critique that virtual communities do not exist in a power vacuum but can in fact be part of new kinds of surveillance by the state and by markets. Information is constantly being collected about Internet users and this amounts to an infringement of the rights of the individual.

Second, related to this liberal stance is the view that virtual communities represent a new kind of commodification of space. While many public bodies are indeed using informational and communication technologies to deliver services to the community, virtual communication is primarily an extension of capitalism. Perhaps not always entirely rejecting the democratizing benefits, concerns are being expressed increasingly about new kinds of dependency and inequality. For instance, it has been estimated that almost half of all Internet users are Americans. The spectre of a 'digital divide' has become a highly topical issue in current debates of information and communication technologies (see DiMaggio *et al.*, 2001; Hargittai, 2002; Norris, 2001).

Third, the view that virtual communities are normless is a common critical position that challenges the democratic thesis. Democracy in a pure form without the rule of law can be dangerous. Many virtual communities are illegal zones in which no moral values operate, as in the case of child pornography or neo-fascist websites. Moreover, it is often claimed that rather than being forms of community in any meaningful sense they are in fact highly individualistic and fragmenting. Thus Cass Sunstein (2001) sees the Internet as a major threat to democracy because of its depersonalizing and filtering of information.

Notwithstanding these objections to virtual community, it can hardly be denied that virtual communities are no less real than other kinds of community and constitute an important dimension of cosmopolitan community more generally. Castells thus refers to the culture of 'real virtuality' to emphasize this.

Cyber-reality is based on a different order of reality than other kinds of reality and consists of a discursively shaped reality perpetuated in movement.

CONCLUSION

The Greek term 'Cyber' derives from the word 'helmsman' who 'pilots' a ship. This is an appropriate metaphor for the current age of mobilities where the individual navigates through global networks of communities beyond the constraints of space and time. This culture of 'real virtuality' has undoubtedly led to forms of empowerment that can vary from the democratization of public services to electronic religions and New Age cults. International non-governmental organizations have been empowered by virtual communities of supporters, but so too have extreme right-wing and ultra-religious groups. Virtual community has the power to construct social and political worlds, for they offer boundless possibilities for both creating and imagining community. But viritual communities, because of their disembodied nature, can be indicative of a withdrawal from community, as Michele Wilson (2002) notes. Because of the strong emphasis on the self in computer-mediated communication, there is a weakening of a commitment to others. Such communities can be only 'thin' and it is unlikely they will generate strong forms of engagement and commitment.

This chapter has stressed the mixed nature of virtual community, both in terms of gains and losses but also the factual reality that viritual community very often exists alongside more spatialized communities. Some of the more extravagant claims made for it have to be questioned in light of recent research which seems to suggest a more complex situation. Communication and information technologies have facilitated the expression of many forms of belonging, ranging from families to political move-ments. Perhaps what is distinctive about virtual community is the enhanced role it gives to communication. Virtual communities are communication communities – they have made belonging more communicative. People are connecting in globalized social networks rather than exclusively in local communal groups and using the new technologies. But this does not mean that place has become irrelevant – computer-mediated communication does not take place in a social vacuum but in social networks. These networks can enhance local forms of belonging rather than undermine them. A tentative conclusion might be that information and communication technologies empower community networks where these already exist but do not, for the most part, create new kinds of community.

CONCLUSION
Theorizing community today

This book has explored the enduring appeal of the idea of community. The modern world has not been only the age of liberty, individualism and reason but has also been marked by a penchant for the cosy world of community, belonging and solidarity where the individual could feel at home in an otherwise homeless and increasingly insecure world. Community has for long been in tension with society, and in recent times disappointment with the promises of the modern state have led to many calls for the revival of community as a basis for politics.

The idea of community seems to suggest a critique of the status quo and thus an alternative to society and the state. Community is, in a sense, an expression of the search for something destroyed by modernity, a quest for an irretrievable past which is irrecoverable because it may have never existed in the first place, as Zygmunt Bauman has argued (Bauman, 2001a). But the search for community cannot be seen only as a backward-looking rejection of modernity, a hopelessly nostalgic plea for the recovery of something lost; it is an expression of very modern values and of a condition that is central to the experience of life today, which we may call the experience of communicative belonging in an insecure world.

Community is becoming more discursively constituted, I have argued. The argument advanced in this book is that contemporary community may be understood as a communication community based on new kinds of belonging. By this is meant a sense of belonging that is peculiar to the circumstances of modern life and which is expressed in unstable, fluid, very open and highly individualized groups. The communities of today are less bounded than those of the very recent past. The communicative ties and cultural structures in the contemporary societies of the global age – as opposed to in industrial and traditional societies – have opened up numerous possibilities for belonging, based on religion, nationalism, ethnicity, lifestyle and gender. It is in this world of plurality rather than of closure that the new kinds of community are emerging.

The persistence of community consists in its ability to communicate ways of belonging, especially in the context of an increasingly insecure world. In this sense, community as belonging is constructed in communicative processes rather than in institutional structures, spaces, or even in symbolic forms of meaning. My focus has been more on belonging than meaning and I emphasized the communicative nature of community as a discourse and a form of experience about belonging as opposed to the emphasis on an underlying sense of morality, a group or place that was characteristic of the older literature on community, much of which in my view has confused the sense of belonging with particular kinds of social organization. Today global forms of communication are offering many opportunities for the construction of community. This leads to an understanding of community that is neither a form of social integration nor one of meaning but is an open-ended system of communication about belonging. Belonging today is participation in communication more than anything else and the multiple forms of communication are mirrored in the plurality of discourses of belonging, which we call communication communities. Neighbourhood communities, such as those in soap operas – *Coronation Street* or *EastEnders* – do not correspond to 'real' communities but are yet more 'real' in their ability to construct a discourse of community. But we must not assert too strongly the novel nature of this. Community has always been based on communication. The traditional 'little community', working-class urban communities, migrant communities and neighbourhoods have all been organized through communicative ties, even if other structures such as symbolic codes and frameworks of authority have played a role. However, the argument advanced here is that today, as communication is becoming more and more freed from the older cultural structures – such as the 'traditional' family, kinship, class – community is becoming receptive to new forms of belonging based on different modes of communication.

Modern society has progressively increased and intensified the search for belonging and has created many new ways of belonging. These ways of belonging differ from group ties in the past in that they are characterized by a stronger communicative component. The individual is not tied to only one community but may have multiple and overlapping bonds; there are more possibilities to enter and exit the group, which may lack continuity over time; and, crucially, the new social bond is tendentially global in its scope due to the growing importance of mediated or indirect social relations. Organized more like a network, community today is abstract and lacks visibility and unity, and as a result is more an imagined condition than a symbolically shaped reality based on fixed reference points. Its boundaries are also more contested and consequently community is also the site of a great deal of conflict. The vitality of community is above all due to its imagined capacity: it is found as much in the search and desire for it than in its capacity to provide enduring forms of symbolic meaning. For this reason I argued that community is more than just symbolically constituted, as anthropologists have argued (Cohen, 1985; Gusfield, 1975; Turner, 1969). It is not merely constituted by the construction of boundaries or legitimated by a higher normative order. Community also has an additional function in the sense that it has to be imagined and does not simply reproduce meaning, but is productive of meaning. Community is indeed not to be confused with institutional structures that attempt to create particular kinds of belonging, as Cohen (1985) correctly argues. As a mode of consciousness it expresses a symbolically constituted level of experience and meaning which is articulated in the construction of boundaries. But to understand community today we need to go beyond the symbolic level of meaning to the additional dimension of the imagined level of group formation. This is because community is not merely about meaning in terms of the symbolic construction of boundaries; it is more about belonging than about boundaries. This point has been established with considerable clarity in recent studies (Amit, 2002; Jodhka, 2002). The building of symbolic boundaries by which self and other are defined is certainly a major part of community and all of group formation, but it is not the only aspect. Equally important is the search for roots and belonging. Especially today, as a result of multiculturalism, polynationality and transnationalism, the differences between groups are becoming more and more diffuse and overlapping. Community is more likely to be expressed in an active search to achieve belonging than in preserving boundaries. Moreover, highly individuated forms of community exist today, and which cannot be compared to the traditional communities of an earlier age. That community is not the opposite to individualism may be illustrated by the fact that participation in many kinds of community requires highly individualized egos who are willing consciously to support collective goals and values. Community today is a product of modernity, not of a premodern traditional world. It presupposes individualism, resilience and a certain reflexivity by which boundaries between self and other are less significant in the making of community. There are post-traditional forms of community, as there are traditional kinds.

Simply put, individuals are not placed into communities only by social forces – which approximates to the view held by Durkheim and by much of classical sociology and anthropology – but they situate themselves in community (Lash, 1994, pp. 146–53). It is not the power of symbolic meanings that distinguishes community but the imagination and the capacity of the self to re-create itself. The symbolic level of community – that is, the dimension of shared meanings by which boundaries are constructed – is thus in tension with the pragmatic role of community as an action system. In addition to its symbolic role, culture is also a form of action. This is more than the symbolic creation of social reality, which is discursively constructed in a communicative process and brings both conflict and consensus along with identity and difference into play. The point is that the community as a symbolic structure exists in a world in which symbolic forms are highly fragmented and are almost always expressed in public media of communication. For this reason they are open to many different kinds of interpretation. It is now more difficult for people in search of community to orient themselves around symbolically coded meanings, such as those that communities in the past could rely on. Of course elites have always manipulated the meaning of symbols but in the past the resonance of the dominant symbolic forms was relatively stable in comparison to the situation today when the new media of communication and other processes of social change, such as globalization, have introduced uncertainty, contingency and dissensus into the symbolic forms of meaning through which community is now being expressed. The symbolic forms of modern life no longer make clear how people should act because these forms have lost their ability to define meaning and have become instead resources for the construction of many different projects. Meaning, in short, is not given but is more and more constructed by a vast variety of social actors who have taken over the symbolic resources of society and are creating new universes of meaning. In other words, community now exists in a meaningless world. It is not the world that is meaningful, but the identity projects of social groups. It is in this essentially communicative world that community is being revived. In going beyond the symbolic approach to community, I am arguing for a more pronounced constructive approach. The notion of community as a 'symbolic construction' suggests a too affirmative sense of community, neglecting its capacity for cultural transformation. It is in this stronger constructivist sense that I argue community is communicative – communicative of new cultural codes of belonging.

The revival of community today is part of a more general tendency towards cultural struggles and conflicts over belonging. Minorities rebel against oppressive majorities and assert their individuality in declarations of identity, solidarity, belonging and roots. Community has been given a major impetus in a world in which everyone can belong to a minority. Postmodern political culture is widely believed to consist of only minorities. Whether in the form of one of the numerous nationalisms, ethnicities, multicultural and communitarian politics, the new and essentially post-traditional assertions of community allow little room for a shared public culture, although they presuppose the possibility of shared values. For this reason, and drawing from postmodern theories of community, I argued that the contemporary resurgence of community is one of radical pluralization (Agamben, 1993; Corlett, 1989; Nancy, 1991). The forms of community are multiple and are expressed in communicative structures that are essentially abstract or imagined – they do not correspond to something clearly visible or to an underlying identity.

This imaginary dimension of community indicates the impossibility of community. Community offers people what neither society nor the state can offer, namely a sense of belonging in an insecure world. But community also destroys this by demonstrating the impossibility of finality. The new kinds of community are themselves, like the wider society, too fragmented and pluralized to offer enduring forms of belonging. Very often the communal spirit is empty of meaning, which must always be individually created. Thus community ends up destroyed by the very individualism that creates the desire for it. Community thus cannot be a basis of social integration, as much of the classical tradition in sociology believed. This myth has been re-created by modern communitarianism which looks to community to provide what neither society nor the state can provide, namely a normatively based kind of social integration rooted in associative principles of a commitment to collective good. As a normative concept community is an important part of modern democracy, providing a civic basis for participation in politics. But this normative concept of community can easily end up as part of the institutional structure of society by becoming an ideology of governance (Rose, 1999). In the extreme, it can become an ideology of total power, as Helmut Plessner has argued in a classic critique of the idea of community (Plessner, [1924] 1999).

Modernity cannot escape the search for community, which may be inescapable as much as it is unattainable, as Peter Wagner argues of the philosophical condition of modernity (Wagner, 2001). The problems of the modern social and political order gave rise to the utopia of a perfect community. From Sir Thomas More through Locke and Rousseau to Marx, modern thought believed in the possibility of political community either within or beyond the state. Much of classical sociological theory hoped modern society might reconcile the condition of the social with community. Today in a post-utopian age, we are less sanguine about this modernist dream. Yet, the vision of a community to come has remained and has become more powerful today. This is not because of nostalgia for something that has been lost but because the question of belonging has become more acute. This is the central argument of this book. Community is relevant today because, on the one side, the fragmentation of society has provoked a worldwide search for community, and on the other, as already argued, cultural developments and global forms of communication have facilitated the construction of community: released from the fetters of traditional social relations in work, family, consumption, the state and education the individual is both more free and at the same time more reliant on alternative social bonds.

With respect to the first point, we may say that globalization, neoliberalism, communication and information technology have not led to greater inclusion. The opposite has been the case, with social exclusion, insecurity and exploitation rising. The social bond has been seriously fragmented as is witnessed by growing concerns about higher levels of violence, stress, suicide and anxiety. Bauman (2000) has called this a 'liquid modernity', a condition in which everything dissolves and is fluid. The atomization of the social has created the conditions for the resurgence of community. On the other side of the double-edged coin that is globalization, it must also be recognized that the emerging structures of the global age provide individuals with many opportunities to build communities in which the promise of belonging may at least be something that can be believed in. The quest for community does not occur in a vacuum but in a world of new technologies.

One aspect of the contemporary kinds of socialization is that it occurs in a mediated form, as opposed to being a direct form of social interaction. The distance between self and other is not necessarily wider but is more mediated by cultural forms which are facilitated by the new technologies of communication. It is in these new and essentially communicative spaces, where a kind of proximity is to be found, that community is created. Proximity is central to the experience of community, and it can take different forms, ranging from culturally intimate forms of de-territorial proximity to more postmodern expressions, as in consumer-mediated kinds of community where culture is not underpinned by territoriality or by common values. Such 'post-modern' forms of community must be seen as imagined rather than as merely symbolic universes of discourse. This is because their capacity to create – what they are presumably intended to create – meaning is limited and because the boundary between self and other is more diffuse.

Because community is imagined does not mean that it is not real. We need to abandon the distinction between real versus imagined community. Territorial kinds of community are different from the new expressions of post-traditional community – virtual communities, New Age communities, gay commu-nities, national and ethnic communities, religious communities – which are also reality-creating forces. Such new kinds of community have a powerful capacity to define new situations and thereby construct social reality. As Cornelius Castoriadis has argued, the radical imaginary is a powerful part of the consti-tution of every social formation and deeply embedded in the psyche and in the social bond (Castoriadis, 1987). While it can frequently take a conservative form affirmative of the status quo, community has also been a radical force. In the terms of Benedict Anderson's theory of imagined community, we may also say that community has an imagined cognitive capacity to define the spheres of life that cannot be grasped in their immediacy (Anderson, 1983). Modern society has increased the range and also the need for such cognitive experiences. For Anderson nationalism is one such example of imagined community. However, we can generalize on this and say that this function is fulfilled by the very idea of community in a great variety of situations. Where national frames of experience and imagination are breaking down, community remains resilient, in many cases providing the basic models, cognitive frames and symbolic resources for the creation of other discourses.

In this view, community is more flexible than may be thought at first sight. Moving away from the traditional conception of community as a territorially located and small-scale unit based on traditional values to a view of community as an expression of the communicative forces within modernity, we arrive at an understanding of community as part of the global world. In the atomization of the social and the erosion of national societies, community has been released and given new life in global forms of communication. A critical perspective cannot be avoided, for the resonance of community in global processes also presents great dangers. While offering a sense of belonging and thus an antidote to the experience of homelessness and insecurity, community is ultimately unable to resist the forces of global-ization, and the alternative it offers is often merely a comfortable illusion based on a communal heaven.

The revival of community today is undoubtedly connected with the crisis of belonging in its relation to place. Globalized communications, cosmopolitan political projects and transna-tional mobilities have given new possibilities to community at precisely the same time that capitalism has undermined the traditional forms of belonging. But these new kinds of commu-nity – which in effect are reflexively organized social networks of individuated members – have not been able to substitute anything for place, other than the aspiration for belonging. Whether community can establish a connection with place, or remain as an imagined condition, will be an important topic for community research in the future.

Notes

1 COMMUNITY AS AN IDEA: LOSS AND RECOVERY

1 This is very well argued by Springborn (1986). See also Frisby and Sayer (1986, pp. 14–16).
2 In *Le Robert Historique*. Cited in Kastoryano (2002, p. 35).
3 See Al-Bayati (1983).
4 See Charles Taylor's interpretation on Hegel and community. ' "Sittlichkeit" refers to the moral obligations I have to an ongoing community of which I am part. . . . The doctrine of Sittlichkeit is that morality reaches its completion in a community' (Taylor, 1994, pp. 376–7).
5 This theme of the incompleteness of community will be stressed continuously throughout this book. It will be demonstrated that this motif is especially central to postmodernist interpretations of community.

2 COMMUNITY AND SOCIETY: MYTHS OF MODERNITY

1 See Calhoun (1980).
2 For this reason the book has also been translated as 'community and association'.
3 See also French (1969) for a collection of some of the major works in this period.

4 See also their later *Culture and Community* (Arensberg and Kimball, 1965).

5 This has been argued by O'Mahony and Delanty (1998).

6 For a good critical discussion of the implications of this for the idea of community, see Cohen (1985, pp. 20–1).

7 His last, and unpublished, work is entitled *The American Societal Community*.

8 See Bell and Newby (1971) and Plant (1974).

9 Turner (1969, chapters 3 and 4); see also Burke (1992, pp. 56–8).

10 See also Black (1997) who has argued that communalism is woven into the history of democracy as much as the idea of individual liberty. Thus when the focus shifts from community as tradition to community as the 'commune', the distinction between community and society becomes more diffuse.

3 URBAN COMMUNITY: LOCALITY AND BELONGING

1 Despite its title, the book was in fact a study of community studies.

2 For an excellent overview of community studies and urban sociology, see Bell and Newby (1971). This book has the added value of including a discussion of community studies in Europe. See also Vidich *et al.* (1964) and, for a more critical analysis of the term, Stacey (1969).

3 On opposition to gentrification, see Abu-Lughod (1994a) and the discussion in the following section of this chapter.

4 On the concept of a housing class, see Moore and Rex (1967).

5 See also Garreau (1991) and Caldeira (1999).

6 Based on a famous article by Norton Long (1958).

7 See also Isin (2000).

8 In an earlier work, *The Uses of Disorder*, Sennett argued that a 'myth of purified community' legitimates racist and exclusionary politics (Sennett, 1970).

9 See also Douglas and Friedmann (1998), Flyvbjerg (1998), Forester (1989).

10 See the debate around Abrams's work (Bulmer, 1986).

11 See also Crow and Allan (1994), Hill (1994) and Mayo (2000) for more on local community development policies.

12 I am drawing from Honneth's work here. See Honneth (2002) where he discusses these issues and also Honneth (1995) and Fraser and Honneth (2001). See Sennet (1998) and Sennet and Cobb (1972). On demoralization, see Febrve (2000) and Bourdieu *et al.* (1999).

13 This was suggested by Gerald Suttles in *The Social Construction of Community* in which he opposed all notions of natural community (Suttles, 1972).

4 POLITICAL COMMUNITY: COMMUNITARIANISM AND CITIZENSHIP

1 I am citing the title of the volume edited by Fred Dallymayr, *From Contract to Community* (Dallymayr, 1978).
2 This is not the only or even the most important aspect of his work, but in terms of communitarian theory it is about where he stands.
3 Sandel (1982), MacIntyre (1981), Selznick (1992) and Taylor (1994, 1990).
4 In this regard I am following the suggestion made in Mulhall and Swift (1996).
5 It should be noted that in American usage 'neoconservatism' is the term generally used for what in British and European usage is 'neoliberalism', both meaning market liberalism. Related to this are the different connotations of liberal and liberalism in American usage where it signifies radical politics as opposed to the conservative politics of conventional republicanism. In this respect it is a contrast to the British/European association of liberal with conservative politics, against which can be distinguished social democracy. In essence, social democracy may be equated with the American usage of liberalism.
6 See *The Politics of Recognition*, the book edited by by Gutmann and containing the often cited papers by Taylor and Habermas among others (Gutmann, 1994).
7 Habermas has been a critic of both liberalism and communitarianism (see Habermas, 1998).
8 See Chapter 6 for a discussion on Habermas' notion of discursive community.
9 See his 1987 essay of that title in Rawls (1993).
10 See Isin and Wood (1999) and Delanty (2000a).
11 See de Tocqueville's classic work *Democracy in America* (1969). See Gittell and Vidal (1998).
12 For criticisms see Whittington (1998) and Cohen (1999).
13 See also Wuthnow (1994), where the emphasis is on community in terms of support groups.

14 As an example of recent, but more civic republican, British communitarianism, see Tan (1998).
15 For a far-reaching critique of communitarianism, see Frazer (1999).

5 COMMUNITY AND DIFFERENCE: VARIETIES OF MULTICULTURALISM

1 This is one of the principal conclusions of a multi-authored work on 'common ground' in contemporary American society (Smelser and Alexander, 1999).
2 The traditional German definition of citizenship through descent, or blood ties, has been softened as a result of recent changes in naturalization laws.
3 I am using the term *liberal communitarian* here in the context of multiculturalism to refer to an essentialy liberal, pluralist conception of multiculturalism that has been in some respects modified by a commitment to community.
4 See also Parekh (2000) for a good definition of multiculturalism in terms of a theory of cultural diversity.

6 COMMUNITIES OF DISSENT: THE IDEA OF COMMUNICATION COMMUNITIES

1 See his theory of the public sphere in Habermas (1996 and 1998). This theory of the public sphere is a development of his earlier one. See Habermas (1989).
2 See his early work on the philosophy of the social sciences (Habermas, 1978). The idea of the scientific community as a communication community is also to be found in Apel (1980).
3 Habermas' critique of communitarianism may be found in Habermas (1994, 1996, 1998). In some of these debates he equates communitarianism with civic republicanism.
4 See Mayo (2000) for a further discussion on community and social movements.
5 On rational choice theory, see Abell (2000).
6 This is also suggested by Robert Wuthnow's idea of 'communities of discourse' (Wuthnow, 1989).

7 POSTMODERN COMMUNITY: COMMUNITY BEYOND UNITY

1 Nancy's book – *La Communauté Déoeuvrée* – appeared in French in 1986 and is titled after an essay published in a French journal in 1893 and which forms the main chapter of the book. The main part of Blanchot's book, 'The Negative Community', was written as a response to Nancy's earlier article and, along with another essay, was published later in French in 1983 as *La Communauté Inavouable*.

2 A tradition that is also based strongly on new readings of Heidegger's philosophy.

3 Readings' book was a critique of the university based on the ideas of Lyotard, Blanchot and Nancy from whom he derived the notion of the community of dissensus.

4 The concept was originally used by Emile Durkheim in *The Elementary Structures of the Religious Life* in 1912 (Durkheim, 1995).

5 The concept of liminality has already been discussed in Chapter 2 to which the reader is referred.

6 Ninety-four people died on British trains between 1988 and 2000 in crashes resulting from lapsed safety.

7 Pahl does not discuss the philosophical literature on friendship that has accompanied the postmodern conceptions of community. Blanchot and Derrida have written works on friendship. See Critchley (1998).

8 COSMOPOLITAN COMMUNITY: BETWEEN THE LOCAL AND THE GLOBAL

1 See also Robertson (1992) and Friedman (1994).

2 This was the title of a famous chapter by Melvin Webber (1963).

3 Urry's book contains an extensive and interesting discussion of new expressions of community. See Chapter 6.

4 Unpublished document in the project 'The Cultural Construction of Communities in the Process of Modernization in Comparison'.

5 The speech was published *The Guardian*, 3 October 2001, pp. 4–5.

6 See Giddens (1998).

7 For a discussion on this see Delanty (2000b).

8 Examples of this approach are Joseph (1999) and Urry (2000).

9 The following discussion on the refugee camp borrows from Peteet's chapter.

9 VIRTUAL COMMUNITY: BELONGING AS COMMUNICATION

1 This has been argued by Wilson (2002).
2 This is not to say that these technologies are not underpinned by hard technologies or that they are less significant.
3 The notion is suggested by Boden and Molotch (1994).
4 A new edition appeared in 2000.
5 See e.g. Bell 2001, pp. 97–100; Slevin 2000, pp. 90–1.

References

Abell, P. (2000) 'Sociological Theory and Rational Choice Theory'. In: Turner, B. S. (ed.) *The Blackwell Companion to Social Theory*. Oxford: Blackwell.

Abu-Lughod, J. (ed.) (1994a) *From Urban Village to East Village: The Battle for New York's Lower East Side*. Oxford: Blackwell.

Abu-Lughod, J. (1994b) 'Conclusions and Implications'. In: Abu-Lughod, J. (ed.) *From Urban Village to East Village: The Battle for New York's Lower East Side*. Oxford: Blackwell.

Agamben, G. (1993) *The Coming Community*. Minneapolis: University of Minnesota Press.

Al-Bayati, B. (1983) *Community and Unity*. London: Academy Editions.

Amit, V. (ed.) (2002) *Realizing Community: Concepts, Social Relationships and Sentiments*. London: Routledge.

Anderson, B. (1983) *Imaginary Communities: Reflections on the Origin and Spread of Nationalism*. London: Verso.

Apel, K.-O. (1980) 'The a priori of the Communication Community and the Foundation of Ethics: The Problem of a Rational Foundation of Ethics in the Scientific Age'. In: Apel, K.-O. *The Transformation of Philosophy*. London: Routledge & Kegan Paul.

Arendt, H. (1958) *The Human Condition*. Chicago, IL: University of Chicago Press.

Arensberg, C. and Kimball, S. (1940/1968) *Family and Community in Ireland*. Cambridge, MA: Harvard University Press.

Arensberg, C. and Kimball, S. (1965) *Culture and Community*. New York: Harcourt, Brace and World.

Armytage, W. (1961) *Heavens Below: Utopian Experiments in England, 1560–1960*. London: Routledge & Kegan Paul.

Augé, M. (1995) *Non-Places: Introduction to an Anthropology of Supermodernity*. London: Routledge.

Barber, B. (1984) *Strong Democracy: Participatory Democracy for a New Age*. Berkeley: University of California Press.

Barber, B. (1996) *Jihad vs. McWorld*. New York: Ballantine Press.

Barth, F. (ed.) (1969) *Ethnic Groups and Boundaries*. London: Allen & Unwin.

Bauböck, R. (2000) 'Liberal Justifications for Ethnic Group Rights'. In: Joppke, C. and Lukes, S. (eds) *Multicultural Questions*. Oxford: Oxford University Press.

Bauman, Z. (1993) *Postmodern Ethics*. Oxford: Blackwell.

Bauman, Z. (2000) *Liquid Modernity*. Cambridge: Polity Press.

Bauman, Z. (2001a) *Community: Seeking Safety in an Insecure World*. Cambridge: Polity Press.

Bauman, Z. (2001b) *The Individualized Society*. Cambridge: Polity Press.

Beck, U. (1997) *The Invention of Politics*. Cambridge: Polity Press.

Beck, U. (1998) *Democracy without Enemies*. Cambridge: Polity Press.

Beck, U. and Beck-Gernsheim, E. (2002) *Individualization*. London: Sage.

Bell, C. and Newby, H. (1971) *Community Studies*. London: Allen & Unwin.

Bell, D. (2001) *An Introduction to Cybercultures*. London: Sage.

Bellah, R., Madsen, R., Sullivan, W., Swidler, A. and Tipton, S. (1996) (2nd edn) *Habits of the Heart*. Berkeley: University of California Press. First published 1986.

Benhabib, S. (1992) *Situating the Self*. Cambridge: Polity Press.

Benhabib, S. (ed.) (1996) *Democracy and Difference: Contesting the Boundaries of the Political*. Princeton, NJ: Princeton University Press.

Black, A. (1997) 'Communal Democracy and its History'. *Political Studies*, 45: 5–20.

Blanchot, M. (1988) *The Unavowable Community*. Barrytown, NY: Station Hill Press.

Boden, D. and Molotch, H. (1994) 'The Compulsion to Proximity'. In: Fridland, R. and Boden, D. (eds) *Now/Where: Time, Space and Modernity*. Berkeley: University of California Press.

Boli, J. and Thomas, G. (1997) 'World Culture in the World Polity: A Century of International Non-Governmental Organization'. *American Sociological Review*, 62: 171–90.

Boli, J. and Thomas, G. (eds) (1999) *Constructing World Culture: International NonGovernmental Organizations since 1875*. Stanford, CA: Stanford University Press.

Borgja, J. and Castells, M. (1997) *Local and Global: Management of Cities in the Information Age*. London: Earthscan.

Bourdieu, P. (1990) *The Logic of Practice*. Cambridge: Polity Press.

Bourdieu, P. *et al.* (1999) *The Weight of the World*. Cambridge: Polity Press.

Bulmer, M. (1986) *Neighbours: The Work of Philip Abrams*. Cambridge: Cambridge University Press.

Burke, P. (1992) *History and Social Theory*. Cambridge: Polity Press.

Burns, L. (2001) 'Derrida and the Promise of Community'. *Philosophy and Social Criticism*, 27 (6): 43–53.

Caldeira, T. (1999) 'Fortified Enclaves: The New Urban Segregation'. In: Holstein, J. (ed.) *Cities and Citizenship*. Durham, NC: Duke University Press.

Calhoun, C. (1980) 'Community: Toward a Variable Conceptualization for Comparative Research'. *Social History*, 5 (1): 105–29.

Calhoun, C. (1982) *The Question of Class Struggle: Social Foundations of Popular Radicalism During the Industrial Revolution*. Chicago, IL: University of Chicago Press.

Calhoun, C. (1983) 'The Radicalness of Tradition: Community Strength or Venerable Disguise and Borrowed Language'. *American Journal of Social Sociology*, 88 (5): 886–914.

Calhoun, C. (1986) 'Computer Technology, Large Scale Social Integration and the Local Community'. *Urban Affairs Quarterly*, 22 (2): 329–49.

Calhoun, C. (1988) 'Populist Politics, Communications Media, and Large Scale Social Integration'. *Sociological Theory*, 6 (2): 219–41.

Calhoun, C. (1991) 'Imagined Communities and Indirect Relationships: Large Scale Social Integration and the Transformation of Everyday Life'. In: Bourdieu, P. and Coleman, J. S. (eds) *Social Theory for a Changing Society*. Boulder, CO: Westview Press.

Calhoun, C. (1992) 'The Infrastructure of Modernity: Indirect Relationships, Information Technology, and Social Integration'. In: Haferkamp, H. and Smelser, N. (eds) *Social Change and Modernity*. Berkeley: University of California Press.

Calhoun, C. (1998) 'Community without Propinquity Revisited: Communications Technology and the Transformation of the Urban Public Sphere'. *Sociological Inquiry*, 68 (3): 373–97.

Castells, M. (1977) *The Urban Question: A Marxist Approach*. London: Arnold.

Castells, M. (1978) *City, Class and Power*. London: Macmillan.

Castells, M. (1983) *The City and the Grassroots*. Berkeley: University of California Press.

Castells, M. (1989) *The Informational City*. Oxford: Blackwell.

Castells, M. (1994) 'European Cities, the Informational Society, and the Global Economy'. *New Left Review*, 204: 18–32.

Castells, M. (1996) *The Information Age*, Vol. 1: *The Rise of the Network Society*. Oxford: Blackwell.

Castells, M. (1997) *The Information Age*, Vol. 2: *The Power of Identity*. Oxford: Blackwell.

Castells, M. (1998) *The Information Age*, Vol. 3: *End of Millennium*. Oxford: Blackwell.

Castells, M. (2001) *The Internet Galaxy: Reflections on the Internet, Business, and Society*. Oxford: Oxford University Press.

Castoriadis, C. (1987) *The Imaginary Institution of Society*. Cambridge: Polity Press.

Cesarani, D. and Fulbrook, M. (eds) (1996) *Citizenship, Nationality and Migration in Europe*. London: Routledge.

Cladis, M. (1992) *A Communitarian Defense of Liberalism: Emile Durkheim and Contemporary Social Theory*. Stanford, CA: Stanford University Press.

Cohen, A. (1985) *The Symbolic Construction of Community*. London: Tavistock.

Cohen, E. (1982) 'Persistence and Change in the Israeli Kibbutz'. In: Kamenka, E. (ed.) *Community as a Social Ideal*. New York: St Martin's Press.

Cohen, J. (1999) 'Does Voluntary Association Make Democracy Work?'. In: Smelser, N. and Alexander, J. (eds) *Diversity and Its Discontents: Cultural Conflict and Common Ground in Contemporary American Society*. New Haven, CT: Princeton University Press.

Cohen, N. (1970) *The Pursuit of the Millennium*. Oxford: Oxford University Press.

Cohen, R. (1997) *Global Diasporas*. London: UCL Press.

Connolly, W. E. (1995) *The Ethos of Pluralization*. Minneapolis: University of Minnesota Press.

Corlett, W. (1989) *Community Without Unity: A Politics of Derridian Extravagance*. Durham, NC: Duke University Press.

Cotterrell, R. (1995) *Law's Community*. Oxford: Clarendon Press.

Critchley, S. (1998) 'The Other's Decision in Me: (What are the Politics of Friendship?)'. *European Journal of Social Theory*, 1 (2): 259–79.

Crow, G. and Allan, G. (1994) *Community Life*. London: Harvester Wheatsheaf.

Dallymayr, F. (ed.) (1978) *From Contract to Community: Political Theory at the Crossroads*. New York: Marcel Dekker.

Dallymayr, F. (1996) 'Democracy and Multiculturalism'. In: Benhabib, S. (ed.) *Democracy and Difference: Contesting the Boundaries of the Political*. Princeton, NJ: Princeton University Press.

Davis, M. (1990) *City of Quartz: Excavating the Future in Los Angeles*. London: Verso.

Davis, M. (1999) *Ecology of Fear: Los Angeles and the Imagination of Disaster*. London: Picador.

Delanty, G. (2000a) *Modernity and Postmodernity: Knowledge, Power, Self*. London: Sage.

Delanty, G. (2000b) *Citizenship in a Global Age: Culture, Society and Politics*. Buckingham: Open University Press.

Delanty, G. (2000c) 'The Resurgence of the City: The Spaces of European Integration'. In: Isin, E. (ed.) *The Politics and City*. London: Routledge.

Delanty, G. (2001) *Challenging Knowledge: The University in the Knowledge Society*. Buckingham: Open University Press.

Delanty, G. and O'Mahony, P. (2002) *Nationalism and Social Theory*. London: Sage.

Della Porta, D. and Diani, M. (1999) *Social Movements: An Introduction*. Oxford: Blackwell.

DiMaggio, P., Hargittai, E., Neuman, W. R. and Robinson, J. P. (2001) 'Social Implications of the Internet'. *Annual Review of Sociology*, 27: 307–36.

Douglas, M. and Friedmann, J. (eds) (1998) *Cities for Citizens: Planning and the Rise of Civil Society in a Global Age*. New York: Wiley.

Durkheim, E. (1957) *Professional Ethics and Civic Morals*. London: Routledge & Kegan Paul.

Durkheim, E. (1964) *The Division of Labour in Society*. Glencoe, IL: The Free Press. First published 1893.

Durkheim, E. (1972) *Emile Durkheim: Selected Writings*. Cambridge: Cambridge University Press.

Durkheim, E. (1995) *The Elementary Structures of the Religious Life*. New York: The Free Press.

Eisenberg, A. (1999) 'Cultural Pluralism Today'. In: Browning, G., Halcli, A. and Webster, F. (eds) *Understanding Contemporary Society: Theories of the Present*. London: Sage.

Eliot, T. S. (1963) *Collected Poems, 1909–1962*. London: Faber and Faber. First published 1922.

Elliott, A. (1999) *Social Theory and Psychoanalysis in Transition: Self and Society from Freud to Kristeva*. London: Free Association Books.

Engels, F. (1936) *The Condition of the Working Class*. London: Unwin Hyman. First published 1845.

Etzioni, A. (1995) *The Spirit of Community*. London: Fontana Press.

Etzioni, A. (2001) *The Monochrome Society*. Princeton, NJ: Princeton University Press.

Evans-Pritchard, E. (1940) *The Nuer*. Oxford: Oxford University Press.

Falk, R. (1995) *On Humane Governance: Toward a New Global Politics*. Cambridge: Polity Press.

Febrve, R. (2000) *The Demoralisation of Western Culture: Social Theory and the Dilemmas of Modern Living*. New York: Continuum.

Fischer, C. (1975) 'Toward a Subcultural Theory of Urbanism'. *American Journal of Sociology*, 80 (1): 319–41.

Fischer, C. (1982) *To Dwell Among Friends: Personal Networks in Town and City*. Chicago, IL: Chicago University Press.

Fischer, C. (1984) *The Urban Experience*. New York: Harcourt, Brace, Jovanovich.

Fischer, C. (1999) 'Uncommon Values, Diversity and Conflict in City Life'. In: Smelser, N. and Alexander, J. (eds) *Diversity and Its Discontents: Cultural Conflict and Common Ground in Contemporary American Society*. Princeton, NJ: Princeton University Press.

Flyvbjerg, B. (1998) *Rationality and Power*. Chicago, IL: University of Chicago Press.

Forester, J. (1989) *Planning in the Face of Power*. Berkeley: University of California Press.

Fowler, R. B. (1991) *The Dance with Community: The Contemporary Debate in American Political Thought*. Lawrence, KN: University Press of Kansas.

Fraser, N. and Honneth, A. (2001) *Recognition or Redistribution? A Political-Philosophical Debate*. London: Verso.

Frazer, E. (1999) *Problems of Communitarian Politics: Unity and Conflict*. Oxford: Oxford University Press.

Frazer, E. and Lacey, N. (1993) *The Politics of Communitarianism: A Feminist Critique of the Liberal Communitarian Debate*. Brighton: Harvester Press.

French, R. M. (ed.) (1969) *The Community: A Comparative Perspective*. Itasca, IL: Peacock Publishing.

Friedman, J. (1994) *Cultural Identity and Global Process*. London: Sage.

Frisby, D. and Sayer, D. (1986) *Society*. London: Tavistock.

Fukuyama, F. (1992) *The End of the History and the Last Man*. Harmondsworth: Penguin.

Gans, H. (1982) *The Urban Villagers*. New York: The Free Press. First published 1962.

Garreau, J. (1991) *Edge City: Life on the New Frontier*. New York: Doubleday.

Gergen, K. (1991) *The Saturated Self*. New York: Basic Books.

Gergen, K. (2001) *Social Construction in Context*. London: Sage.

Giddens, A. (1990) *The Consequences of Modernity*. Cambridge: Polity Press.

Giddens, A. (1991) *Modernity and Self-Identity*. Cambridge: Polity Press.

Giddens, A. (1994) *Beyond Left and Right*. Cambridge: Polity Press.

Giddens, A. (1998) *The Third Way: The Renewal of Social Democracy*. Cambridge: Polity Press.

Gittell, R. and Vidal, A. (1998) *Communal Organizing: Building Social Capital as a Developmental Strategy*. London: Sage.

Glazer, N. (1997) *We Are All Multiculturalists Now*. Cambridge, MA: Harvard University Press.

Glazer, N. (2000) 'Multiculturalism and American Exceptionalism'. In: Joppke, C. and Lukes, S. (eds) *Multicultural Questions*. Oxford: Oxford University Press.

Glazer, N. and Moynihan, D. (1963) *Beyond the Melting Pot*. Cambridge, MA: MIT Press.

Goldberg, D. (ed.) (1994) *Multiculturalism: A Reader*. Oxford: Oxford University Press.

Goodman, P. (1960) *Communitas: Means of Livelihood and Ways of Life*. New York: Vintage Books.

Gronow, J. (1997) *The Sociology of Taste*. London: Routledge.

Gusfield, J. (1975) *Community: A Critical Response*. Oxford: Blackwell.

Gutmann, A. (1993) 'The Challenge of Multiculturalism in Political Ethics'. *Philosophy and Public Affairs*, 22 (3): 171–206.

Gutmann, A. (ed.) (1994) *Multiculturalism: Examining the Politics of Recognition*. Princeton, NJ: Princeton University Press.

Habermas, J. (1978) *Knowledge and Human Interests* (2nd edn). London: Heinemann.

Habermas, J. (1984) *The Theory of Communicative Action*, Vol. 1: *Reason and the Rationalization of Society*. London: Heinemann.

Habermas, J. (1987) *The Theory of Communicative Action*, Vol. 2: *Lifeworld and System: A Critique of Functionalist Reason*. Cambridge: Polity Press.

Habermas, J. (1989) *The Structural Transformation of the Public Sphere*. Cambridge: Polity Press.

Habermas, J. (1994) 'Struggles for Recognition in the Democratic Constitutional State'. In: Gutmann, A. (ed.) *Multiculturalism: Examining the Politics of Recognition*. Princeton, NJ: Princeton University Press.

Habermas, J. (1996) *Between Facts and Norms: Contributions to a Discourse Theory of Law and Democracy*. Cambridge: Polity Press.

Habermas, J. (1998) *The Inclusion of the Other: Studies in Political Theory*. Cambridge, MA.: MIT Press.

Hall, J. A. and Lindholm, C. (1999) *Is America Breaking Apart?* Princeton, NJ: Princeton University Press.

Hargittai, E. (2002) 'Second-Level Digital Divide: Differences in People's Online Skills'. *First Monday*. Http://firstmonday.org/issues/issue/_4/ hargittai/.

Harvey, D. (1990) *The Condition of Postmodernity: An Inquiry into the Origins of Cultural Change*. Oxford: Blackwell.

Heelas, P. (1996) *The New Age Movement: The Celebration of the Self and the Sacralization of Modernity*. Oxford: Blackwell.

Held, D. (1995) *Democracy and the Global Order: From the Modern State to Cosmopolitan Governance*. Cambridge: Polity Press.

Hetherington, K. (2000) *New Age Travellers*. London: Cassell.

Hill, C. (1975) *The World Turned Upside Down*. London: Penguin Books.

Hill, D. (1994) *Citizens and Cities*. London: Harvester Wheatsheaf.

Hirst, P. (1994) *Associative Democracy: New Forms of Economic and Social Governance*. Cambridge: Polity Press.

Hobsbawm, E. (1994) *The Age of Extremes: The Short Twentieth Century, 1914–1991*. London: Michael Joseph.

Hollinger, D. (1995) *Postethnic America: Beyond Multiculturalism*. New York: Basic Books.

Honneth, A. (1995) *The Struggle for Recognition*. Cambridge: Polity Press.

Honneth, A. (2002) 'An Interview with Axel Honneth: the Role of Sociology in the Theory of Recognition'. *The European Journal of Social Theory*, 5(2): 265–77.

Isin, E. (ed.) (2000) *Democracy, Citizenship and the Global City*. London: Routledge.

Isin, E. and Wood, P. (1999) *Citizenship and Identity*. London: Sage.

Jacoby, R. (1999) *The End of Utopia: Politics and Culture in an Age of Apathy*. New York: Basic Books.

Jameson, F. (1991) *Postmodernism, or, the Cultural Logic of Late Capitalism*. Durham, NC: Duke University Press.

Joas, H. (1998) 'The Autonomy of the Self: The Meadian Heritage and its Postmodern Challenge'. *European Journal of Social Theory*, 1 (1): 7–18.

Jodhka, S. (ed.) (2002) *Community and Identity: Contemporary Discourses on Cultures and Politics in India*. New Delhi and London: Sage.

Jones, S. (ed.) (1995) *Cybersociety: Computer Mediated Communication and Community*. London: Sage.

Joseph, M. (1999) *Nomadic Identities: The Performance of Citizenship*. Minneapolis: University of Minnesota Press.

Kamenka, E. (ed.) (1982a) *Community as a Social Ideal*. New York: St Martin's Press.

Kamenka, E. (1982b) 'Community and the Socialist Idea'. In: Kamenka, E. (ed.) *Community as a Social Ideal*. New York: St Martin's Press.

Kant, I. (1952) *The Critique of Judgement*. Oxford: Oxford University Press. First published 1790.

Kastoryano, R. (2002) *Negotiating Identity: States and Immigration in France and Germany*. Princeton, NJ: Princeton University Pres.

König, R. (1968) *The Community*. London: Routledge & Kegan Paul.

Kumar, T. (1987) *Utopia and Anti-Utopia in Modern Times*. Oxford: Blackwell.

Kymlicka, W. (1989) *Liberalism, Community and Culture*. Oxford: Clarendon Press.

Kymlicka, W. (1995) *Multicultural Citizenship: A Liberal Theory of Minority Rights*. Oxford: Clarendon Press.

Kymlicka, W. (1996) 'Three Forms of Group-Differentiated Citizenship in Canada'. In: Benhabib, S. (ed.) *Democracy and Difference: Contesting the Boundaries of the Political*. Princeton, NJ: Princeton University Press.

Lasch, C. (1979) *The Culture of Narcissism*. New York: Norton.

Lasch, C. (1995) *The Revolt of the Elites and the Betrayal of Democracy*. New York: Norton.

Lasch, C. (2002) *Critique of Information*. London: Sage.

Lash, S. (1994) 'Reflexivity and its Doubles: Structures, Aesthetics, Community'. In: Beck, U., Giddens, A. and Lash, S. *Reflexive Modernization: Politics, Tradition and Aesthetics in the Modern Social Order*. Cambridge: Polity Press.

Lazare, D. (1996) *The Frozen Republic: How the Constitution is Paralyzing Democracy*. New York: Harcourt.

Le Bon, G. (1995) *The Crowd*. New Brunswick, NJ: Transaction Publishers.

Lichterman, P. (1996) *The Search for Political Community: American Activists Reinventing Commitment*. Cambridge: Cambridge University Press.

Lindroos, K. (2001) 'Scattering Community: Benjamin on Experience, Narrative and History'. *Philosophy and Social Criticism*, 27 (6): 19–41.

Lister, R. (1997) *Citizenship: Feminist Perspectives*. London: Macmillan.

Lister, R. (1998) 'Citizenship and Difference: Towards a Differentiated Universalism'. *European Journal of Social Theory*, 1 (1): 71–90.

Long, N. (1958) 'The Local Community as an Ecology of Games'. *American Journal of Sociology*, 64: 251–61.

Lynd, R. and Lynd, H. (1929) *MiddleTown*. New York: Harcourt-Brace.

Lynd, R. and Lynd, H. (1937) *MiddleTown in Transition*. New York: Harcourt-Brace.

MacIntyre, A. (1981) *After Virtue*. London: Duckworth.

McLuhan, M. (1962) *The Gutenberg Galaxy: The Making of Typographic Man*. Toronto: University of Toronto Press.

MacPherson, C. P. (1962) *The Political Theory of Possessive Individualism*. Oxford: Clarendon Press.

Maffesoli, M. (1996a) *The Time of the Tribes: The Decline of Individualism in Mass Society*. London: Sage.

Maffesoli, M. (1996b) *The Contemplation of the World*. Minneapolis: Minnesota University Press.

Maine, H. S. (1895) *Village Communities in the East and West* (7th edn). London: Murray. First published 1861.

Maine, H. S. (1905) *Ancient Law: Its Connection with the Early History of Society and its Relation to Modern Times* (10th edn). London: Murray. First published 1861.

Mayo, M. (2000) *Cultures, Communities, Identities*. London: Palgrave.

Melucci, A. (1996a) *Challenging Codes: Collective Action in the Information Age*. Cambridge: Cambridge University Press.

Melucci, A. (1996b) *The Playing Self: Person and Meaning in the Planetary Society*. Cambridge: Cambridge University Press.

Miller, D. (1989) *Markets, the State and Community*. Oxford: Oxford University Press.

Miller, D. and Walzer, M. (eds) (1995) *Pluralism, Justice, and Equality*. Oxford: Oxford University Press.

Mollenkopf, J. and Castells, M. (1991) *Dual City: Restructuring New York*. New York: Russell Sage Foundation.

Moore, R. (1974) *Pit-Men, Preachers, and Politics: The Effects of Methodism in a Durham Mining Community*. Cambridge: Cambridge University Press.

Moore, R. (1982) *The Social Impact of Oil: The Case of Peterhead*. London: Routledge & Kegan Paul.

Moore, R. and Rex, J. (1967) *Race, Community and Conflict*. Oxford: Oxford University Press.

Morris, P. (1996) 'Community Beyond Tradition'. In: Hellas, P., Lash, S. and Morris, P. (eds) *Detraditionalization*. Oxford: Blackwell.

Mosse, G. (1982) 'Nationalism, Fascism and the Radical Right'. In: Kamenka, E. (ed.) *Community as a Social Ideal*. New York: St Martin's Press.

Mulhall, S. and Swift, A. (1996) *Liberalism and Communitarianism* (2nd edn). Oxford: Blackwell.

Nancy, J.-L. (1991) *The Inoperative Community*. Minneapolis: University of Minnesota Press.

Nederveen Pieterse, J. (1997) 'Traveling Islam: Mosques without Minarets'. In: Öncu, A. and Weyland, P. (eds) *Space, Culture and Power*. London: Zed Books.

Nisbet, R. (1953) *The Quest for Community*. Oxford: Oxford University Press.

Nisbet, R. (1967) *The Sociological Tradition*. London: Heinemann.

Norris, P. (2001) *Digital Divide: Civic Engagement, Information Poverty and the Internet in Democratic Societies*. Cambridge: Cambridge University Press.

O'Mahony, P. and Delanty, G. (1998) *Rethinking Irish History: Nationalism, Identity and Ideology*. London: Macmillan.

O'Neill, J. (1994) *The Missing Child of Liberal Theory: Towards a Covenant Theory of Family, Community, Welfare and the Civic State*. Toronto: University of Toronto Press.

Offe, C. (1998) ' "Homogeneity" and Constitutional Democracy: Coping with Identity Conflicts through Group Rights'. *Journal of Political Philosophy*, 6(2): 113–57.

Oldfield, M. (1990) *Citizenship and Community: Civic Republicanism and the Modern World*. London: Routledge.

Ong, A. (1999) *Flexible Citizenship: The Cultural Logics of Transnationality*. Durham, NC: Duke University Press.

Pahl, R. (1995) *After Success: Fin-de-Siècle Anxiety and Identity*. Cambridge: Polity Press.

Pahl, R. (2001) *On Friendship*. Cambridge: Polity Press.

Parekh, B. (2000) *Rethinking Multiculturalism: Cultural Diversity and Political Theory*. London: Macmillan.

Park, R. (1915) 'The City: Suggestions for the Investigation of Human Behaviour in the City'. *American Journal of Sociology*, 20: 577–612.

Park, R. (1952) *Human Communities*. Glencoe, IL: The Free Press.

Parsons, T. (1951) *The Social System*. New York: The Free Press.

Parsons, T. (1960) 'The Principal Structures of Community'. In: Parsons, T. *Structure and Process in Modern Society*. Glencoe, IL: The Free Press.

Parsons, T. (1961) *Societies: Evolutionary and Comparative Perspectives*. Englewood Cliffs, NJ: Prentice-Hall.

Pawley, M. (1973) *The Private Future: Causes and Consequences of Community Collapse in the West*. London: Thames and Hudson.

Perea, J. (ed.) (1996) *Immigrants Out! The New Nativism and the Anti-Immigrant Impulse in the United States*. New York: New York University Press.

Peteet, J. (2000) 'Refugees, Resistance, and Identity'. In Guidry, J., Kennedy, M. and Zald, M. (eds) *Globalization and Social Movements: Culture, Power, and the Transnational Public Sphere*. Ann Arbor, MI: The University of Michigan Press.

Plant, R. (1974) *Community and Ideology: An Essay in Applied Social Philosophy*. London: Routledge & Kegan Paul.

Plessner, H. (1999) *The Limits of Community*. New York: Humanities Books. First published 1924.

Pocock, J. G. A. (1995) 'The Ideal of Citizenship since Modern Times'. In: Beiner, R. (ed.) *Theorizing Citizenship*. New York: SUNY Press.

Poster, M. (1995) *The Second Media Age*. Cambridge: Polity Press.

Putnam, R. (1993) *Making Democracy Work: Civic Traditions in Modern Italy*. Princeton, NJ: Princeton University Press.

Putnam, R. (1999) *Bowling Alone*. New York: Simon & Schuster.

Rawls, J. (1971) *A Theory of Justice*. Cambridge, MA: Harvard University Press.

Rawls, J. (1993) *Political Liberalism*. New York: Columbia University Press.

Rawls, J. (1999) *A Law of Peoples*. Cambridge, MA: Harvard University Press.

Readings, B. (1996) *The University in Ruins*. Cambridge, MA: Harvard University Press.

Redfield, R. (1955) *The Little Community*. Chicago, IL: University of Chicago Press.

Rheingold, H. (1993) *The Virtual Community: Homesteading on the Electronic Frontier*. Reading, MA: Addison-Wesley.

Robertson, R. (1992) *Globalization: Social Theory and Global Culture*. London: Sage.

Rose, N. (1999) *Powers of Freedom*. Cambridge: Cambridge University Press.

Rousseau, J.-J. (1968) *The Social Contract*. Harmondsworth: Penguin. First published 1762.

Sandel, M. (1982) *Liberalism and the Limits of Justice*. Cambridge: Cambridge University Press.

Sandercock, L. (1998) *Towards Cosmopolis: Planning for the Multicultural Cities*. New York: John Wiley.

Sassen, S. (1992) *The Global City: New York, London, Tokyo*. Princeton, NJ: Princeton University Press.

Sassen, S. (1996) *Losing Control: Sovereignty in an Age of Globalization*. New York: Columbia University Press.

Sassen, S. (1999) *Guests and Aliens*. New York: New Press.

Sassen, S. (2002) 'Toward a Sociology of Information Technology'. *Current Sociology*, 50 (3): 365–88.

Schain, M. (2000) 'Minorities and Immigrant Incorporation in France: The State and the Dynamics of Multiculturalism'. In: Joppke, C. and Lukes, S. (eds) *Multicultural Questions*. Oxford: Oxford University Press.

Schefer-Huges, N. (1992) *Death without Weeping: The Violence of Everyday Life in Brazil*. Berkeley: University of California Press.

Schlesinger, A. (1992) *The Disuniting of America*. New York: Norton.

Schmalenbach, H. (1977) *On Society and Experience: Selected Papers*, edited, translated, and with an Introduction by G. Lüschen and G. P. Stone. Chicago, IL: Chicago University Press.

Schwartz, B. (1991) 'Chinese Culture and the Concept of Community'. In: Rouner, L. (ed.) *On Community*. Notre Dame: University of Notre Dame Press.

Selznick, P. (1992) *The Moral Commonwealth: Social Theory and the Promise of Community*. Berkeley: University of California Press.

Sennett, R. (1970) *The Uses of Disorder*. New York: Knopf.

Sennett, R. (1978) *The Fall of Public Man*. New York: Vintage.

Sennett, R. (1998) *The Corrosion of Character: The Personal Consequences of Work in the New Capitalism*. New York: Norton.

Sennett, R. and Cobb, J. (1972) *The Hidden Injuries of Class*. Cambridge: Cambridge University Press.

Shields, R. (1991) *Places on the Margin: Alternative Geographies of Modernity*. London: Routledge.

Shields, R. (ed.) (1996) *Cultures of the Internet*. London: Sage.

Simmel, G. (1950) 'The Metropolis and Mental Life'. In: Wolff, K. (ed.) *The Sociology of Georg Simmel*. New York: The Free Press. First published 1905.

Simmel, G. (1955) *Conflict and the Web of Group Affiliations*. Glencoe, IL: The Free Press.

Slevin, J. (2000) *The Internet and Society*. Cambridge: Polity Press.

Smelser, N. and Alexander, J. (eds) (1999) *Diversity and Its Discontents: Cultural Conflict and Common Ground in Contemporary American Society*. Princeton, NJ: Princeton University Press.

Smith, M. and Kollock, P. (eds) (1999) *Communities in Cyberspace*. London: Routledge.

Smith, N. (1996) *The New Urban Frontier: Gentrification and the Revanchist City*. London: Routledge.

Soja, E. (1996) *Thirdspace: Journeys to Los Angeles and Other Real and Imagined Places*. Oxford: Blackwell.

Soysal, Y. N. (1994) *Limits of Citizenship: Migrants and Postnational Membership in Europe*. Chicago, IL: Chicago University Press.

Spivak, G. (1987) *In Other Words*. London: Routledge.

Springborn, P. (1986) 'Politics, Primordialism, and Orientalism: Marx, Aristotle, and the Myth of the Gemeinschaft'. *American Political Science Review*, 80 (1): 185–211.

Stacey, M. (1960) *Tradition and Change: A Study of Banbury*. Oxford: Oxford University Press.

Stacey, M. (1969) 'The Myth of Community Studies'. *British Journal of Sociology*, 20 (2): 134–47.

Stallybrass, P. and White, A. (1986) *The Politics and Poetics of Transgression*. London: Methuen.

Stedman Jones, S. (2001) *Durkheim Reconsidered*. Cambridge: Polity Press.

Stein, M. (1960) *The Eclipse of Community*. Princeton, NJ: Princeton University Press.

Steinberg, S. (1989) *The Ethnic Myth*. New York: Beacon.

Strydom, P. (2002) *Risk, Environment and Society*. Buckingham: Open University Press.

Sunstein, C. (2001) *Republic.com*. Princeton, NJ: Princeton University Press.

Suttles, G. (1968) *The Social Order of the Slum: Ethnicity and Territory in the Inner City*. Chicago, IL: Chicago University Press.

Suttles, G. (1972) *The Social Construction of Communities*. Chicago, IL: University of Chicago Press.

Tan, H. (1998) *Communitarianism: A New Agenda for Politics and Citizenship*. London: Macmillan.

Taylor, C. (1975) *Hegel*. Cambridge: Cambridge University Press.

Taylor, C. (1990) *Sources of the Self*. Cambridge, MA: Harvard University Press.

Taylor, C. (1994) 'The Politics of Recognition'. In: Gutmann, A. (ed.) *Multiculturalism: Examining the Politics of Recognition*. Princeton, NJ: Princeton University Press.

Thompson, J. (1998) 'Community Identity and World Citizenship'. In Archibugi, D., Held, D. and Köhler, M. (eds) *Re-imagining Political Community*. Oxford: Blackwell.

Tocqueville, A. de (1969) *Democracy in America*. New York: Doubleday. First published in 2 vols, 1835 and 1840.

Tönnies, F. (1963) *Community and Society*. New York: Harper and Row.

Touraine, A. (1995) *Critique of Modernity*. Oxford: Blackwell.

Touraine, A. (1997) *What is Democracy?* Oxford: Westview Press.

Touraine, A. (2000) *Can We Live Together? Equal and Different*. Cambridge: Polity Press.

Trend, D. (1997) *Cultural Democracy*. New York: State University of New York Press.

Tully, J. (1995) *Strange Multiplicities: Constitutionalism in an Age of Diversity*. Cambridge: Cambridge University Press.

Turner, B. (2001) 'Outline of a General Theory of Cultural Citizenship'. In: Stevenson, N. (ed.) *Culture and Citzenship*. London: Sage.

Turner, V. (1969) *The Ritual Process: Structure and Anti-Structure*. London: Routledge & Kegan Paul.

Upadhya, C. (2002) 'The Concept of Community in Indian Social Sciences: An Anthropological Perspective'. In Jodhka, S. (ed.) *Community and Identities: Contemporary Discourses on Culture and Politics in India*. New Delhi and London: Sage.

Urban, G. (1996) *Metaphysical Community: The Intellect and the Senses*. Austin: University of Texas Press.

Urry, J. (2000) *Sociology Beyond Societies: Mobilities for the Twenty-First Century*. London: Routledge.

Van Gennep, A. (1960) *The Rites of Passage*. London: Routledge & Kegan Paul.

Vidich, A., Bensman, J. and Stein, M. (eds) (1964) *Reflections on Community Studies*. New York: John Wiley.

Wacquant, L. (1992) 'The Comparative Structure and Experience of Urban Exclusion: "Race", Class, and Space in Paris and Chicago'. In: McFate, K. *et al.* (eds) *Poverty, Inequality and the Future of the Social Policy*. New York: Russell Sage Foundation.

Wacquant, L. (1993) 'Urban Outcasts: Stigma and Division in the Black American Ghetto and French Urban Periphery'. *International Journal of Urban and Regional Research*, 17 (3): 366–83.

Wacquant, L. (1999) 'America as Social Dystopia: The Politics of Urban Disintegration, or the French Use of the "American Model"'. In: Pierre Bourdieu *et al. The Weight of the World: Social Suffering in Contemporary Society*. Cambridge: Polity Press.

Wagner, P. (2001) *Theorizing Modernity*. London: Sage.

Walzer, M. (1983) *Spheres of Justice*. New York: Basic Books.

Walzer, M. (1994) *Thick and Thin: Moral Argument at Home and Abroad*. Notre Dame: Notre Dame University Press.

Watson, C. W. (2000) *Multiculturalism*. Buckingham: Open University Press.

Webber, M. (1963) 'Order in Diversity: Community without Propinquity'. In: Wingo, L. (ed.) *Cities and Space: The Future Use of Urban Land*. Baltimore, MD: Johns Hopkins University Press.

Weber, M. (1947) *Social and Economic Organization*. New York: The Free Press.

Weber, M. (1958) *The City*. New York: The Free Press. First published 1905.

Wellman, B. (1979) 'The Community Question'. *American Journal of Sociology*, 84: 1201–31.

Wellman, B. (2001) 'Physical Place and Cyberplace: The Rise of Networked Individualism'. *International Journal of Urban and Regional Research*, 25(2): 227–52.

Wellman, B. and Leighton, B. (1979) 'Networks, Neighbourhoods, and Communities: Approaches to the Study of the Community Question'. *Urban Affairs Quarterly*, 14: 363–90.

Whittington, K. (1998) 'Revisiting Tocqueville's America: Society, Politics, and Association in the Nineteenth Century'. *American Behavioral Scientist*, 42 (1): 21–32.

Whyte, W. F. (1943) *Street Corner Society*. Chicago, IL: University of Chicago Press.

Whyte, W. H. (1957) *The Organization Man*. New York: Doubleday Anchor Books.

Wieviorka, M. (1998) 'Is Multiculturalism the Solution?' *Ethnic and Racial Studies*, 21 (5): 881–910.

Williams, P. and Smith, N. (eds) (1986) *Gentrification and the City*. London: Allen & Unwin.

Williams, R. (1961) *Culture and Society*. London: Penguin.

Williams, R. (1976) *Keywords: A Vocabulary of Culture and Society*. London: Penguin.

Wilson, M. (2002) 'Community in the Abstract: A Political and Ethical Dilemma?' In: Bell, D. and Kennedy, B. (eds) *The CyberCultures Reader*. London: Routledge.

Wirth, L. (1938) 'Urbanism as a Way of Life'. *American Journal of Sociology*, 44 (1): 1–24.

Wrong, D. (1961) 'The Oversocialized Conception of Man in Modern Sociology'. *American Sociological Review*, 26: 183–93.

Wuthnow, R. (1989) *Communities of Discourse: Ideology and Social Structure in the Reformation, The Enlightenment, and European Socialism*. Cambridge, MA: Harvard University Press.

Wuthnow, R. (1994) *Sharing the Journey: Support Groups and America's New Quest for Community*. New York: The Free Press.

Young, I. M. (1989) 'Polity and Group Difference: A Critique of the Ideal of Universal Citizenship'. *Ethics*, 99: 250–74.

Young, I. M. (1990) *Justice and the Politics of Difference*. Princeton, NJ: Princeton University Press.

Young, I. M. (2000) *Inclusion and Democracy*. Oxford: Oxford University Press.

Young, M. and Willmott, P. (1957) *Family and Kinship in East London*. London: Penguin.

INDEX